NBANBANBANBANBANBANBA

EXTERNAL WORKS
DETAIL SHEETS

National Building Agency

The Architectural Press Ltd: London
Nichols Publishing Company: New York

First published in 1977 by
The Architectural Press Ltd, London
© 1977 National Building Agency
All rights reserved. No part of this
publication may be reproduced or
photocopied for commercial use without
the prior permission of the publishers.
Such permission, if granted, is subject
to a fee depending on the nature of the use.

ISBN O 85139 215 6 (cloth) (British edition)
ISBN O 85139 214 8 (paper) (British edition)

First published in the United States in 1977 by
Nichols Publishing Company
175 West 79th Street
Post Office Box 96
New York, N.Y. 10024

Library of Congress Cataloging in Publication Data

National Building Agency

   External works detail sheets

   1. Architecture--Details. 2. Building--Details.

1. Title.

NA2840.N3 1977   729   77-138

ISBN O-89397-020-4 (USA edition)

Printed in Great Britain by
R. J. Acford Ltd, Industrial Estate, Chichester, Sussex

CONTENTS

Foreword by Cleeve Barr
(Managing Director, National Building Agency)

FOREWORD

This publication offers professional practices and other design offices the nucleus of a library of external works Detail Sheets, which can be extended, on a comparative format, according to the experience and wishes of each individual practice.

For those who find in it exactly the details they want it offers a comparative cost index, references to British Standards and suggestions for cross-referencing to and preparing layout drawings - with consequent savings in time and with consistent specification and presentation.

For all practices, it offers a means of consistently filing and comparing external works details (with cost indices and source references) within which it is easy to incorporate feedback, to amend details and to add (or delete) alternatives to build up an individual office vocabulary.

Each design office will develop its own way of using these Detail Sheets. I hope they prove useful - and that future editions will benefit from contributions from readers' own experience.

Cleeve Barr.

EXTERNAL WORKS DETAIL SHEETS

Introduction

External works detail sheets have been introduced in an effort to cut out needless repetition of effort in detailing external works.

It is possible to use the detail sheets without alteration if the detail fits the requirements of the job. However, in most cases, minor modifications and additions to the dimensions or specification will be necessary.

When a detail is required which is not available on a detail sheet (and there will be many) the new detail is drawn by the designer using a standardised format which will enable it to be added to the original collection of details and to be easily re-used on other jobs. The original collection will thus be enlarged and enriched by new details particular to a practice.

Users of this book are invited to send the publishers copies of their own details which they think would merit inclusion in future editions of this book.

Each sheet portrays a detail without reference to its surroundings. This approach is adopted because it affords to each detail the maximum number of possibilities for re-use. No attempt is made to recommend a particular detail for a particular situation. This remains the responsibility of the Job Architect.

The design notes which precede each section are intended to give only the briefest outline of main points. For more detailed design guidance the publications listed at the end of the design notes should be consulted. Details should not be used without a knowledge of the content of the British Standards contained in the specification. Some British Standards contain alternative specifications which might be more suitable in a particular case.

Use of the Detail Sheets

It is intended that the original collection of Detail Sheets, as purchased, should be broken down into individual leaves, punched, and stored in a ring binder. The Detail Sheets are bound together in a way which will facilitate this operation.

In the form of individual leaves the details can be easily photo-copied and traced.

The sheets must be used in conjunction with a site layout drawing preferably at 1:200. The layout drawing will convey all information on levels, direction of falls, setting out dimension for walls and paths, and location of posts, piers and construction joints.

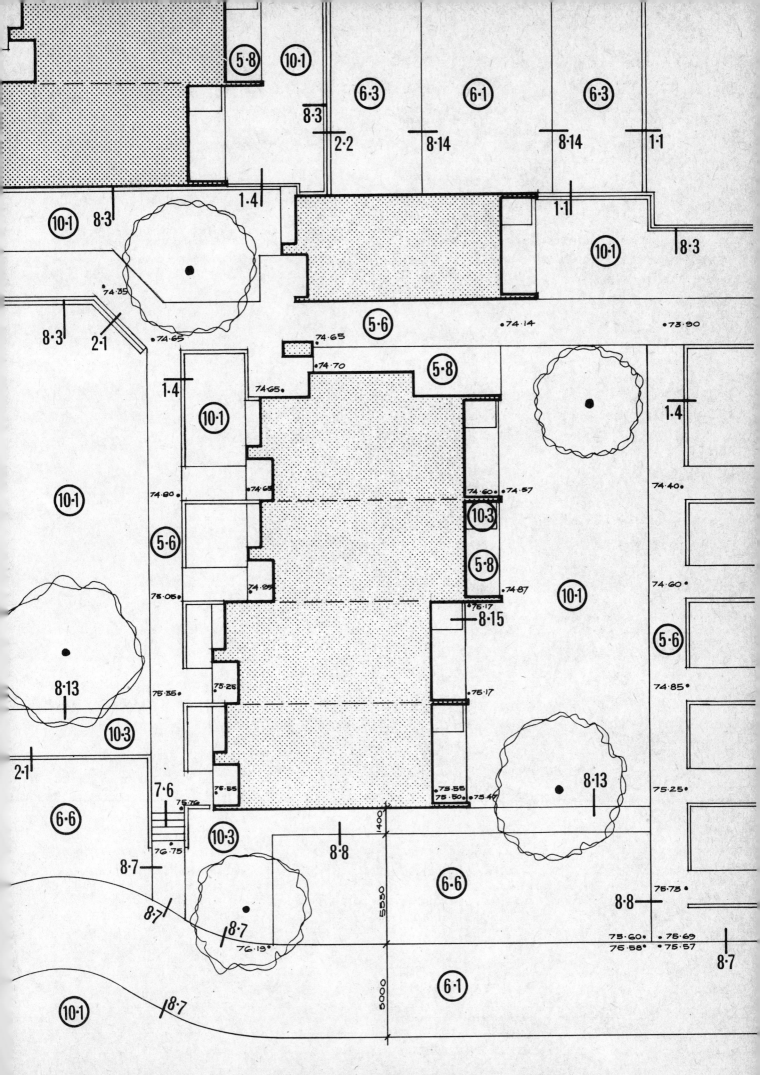

FIGURE 1 Layout Drawing

The layout drawing will also indicate the location of the selected details and the deployment of surface finishes. (See Figure 1).

Linear constructions (walls, fences, kerbs, etc.) are indicated by a section line in conjunction with the detail reference number. (See Figure 2).

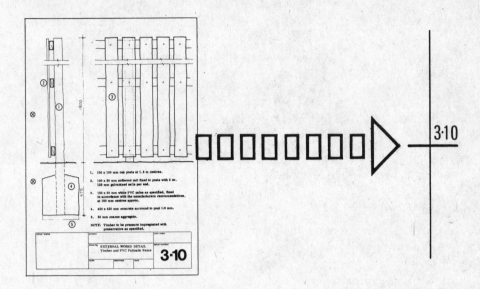

FIGURE 2 Linear Constructions

Planar constructions (pavings, roads, topsoiling, etc.) are indicated by the detail reference number enclosed in a circle. (See Figure 3).

Where two planar constructions meet without the introduction of a third element such as a kerb or an edging, there is no need for further detail at the junction. Any required difference in levels can be indicated on the layout drawing by figured levels.

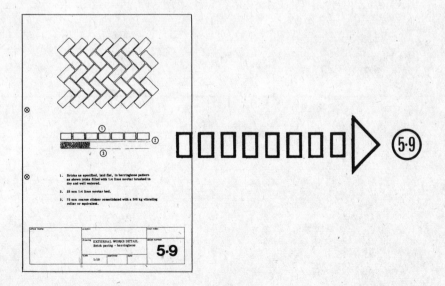

FIGURE 3 Planar Constructions

Care should be taken to indicate on the layout drawing the precise boundaries of planar constructions and the extent of linear constructions.

If considered necessary perspective sketches can be used where a particular conjunction of details needs more detailed explanation.

Simple conjunction of details, for example a wall and a mowing strip, can be indicated by the drawing of the two relevant section lines in close proximity.   (See Figure 4).

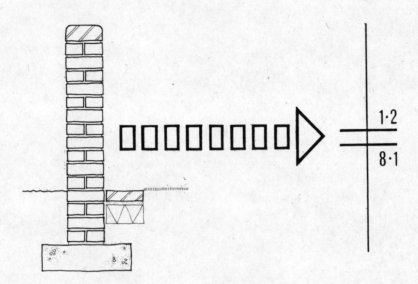

FIGURE 4 Conjunction of Details

Standards

British Standards and Codes of Practice are referred to, where necessary, both in the text and on the details.   Users of this book living in countries where British Standards are not used should delete the reference to the British Standard and, if they then feel it necessary, should either insert a reference to an equivalent national standard or describe what is required in empirical terms.

Cost Index

Each detail has been given a cost index to roughly indicate comparative costs within each functional group, ie Walls, Fences, etc.

The least expensive construction in each group is assigned the cost index of 100.   Thus a detail bearing an index of 250 will be two and a half times as expensive as the detail bearing the index of 100 and half as expensive as a detail bearing an index of 500.

The indices are based on prices quoted by manufacturers and published in pricing reference manuals at the time of printing.   However, although actual prices may change quite rapidly from year to year, the cost indices will remain static, and only change when the price of a particular material increases faster than the norm.

For external walls the cost of facing bricks has been assumed as £50 per thousand, excluding delivery.   For other materials local deliveries have been assumed.

Any new detail can quickly be given a cost index by reference to any of the original details the cost of which is known in monetary terms.

Issue of Detail Sheets

Detail sheets can be used in two ways:

The first is to issue to the contractor a set of photo-copies of the selected details, after completion of the title panel and stamping each detail with the office stamp.

The second method is to trace each detail onto an AI sheet of tracing paper and include the drawing with the contract set in the normal way.   (See Figure 5).

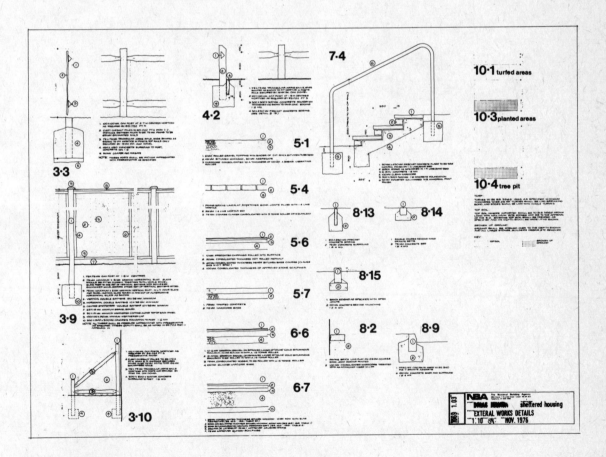

FIGURE 5   Details traced onto A1 sheet

Production of New Detail Sheets

Where the use of a detail not included in the original collection of Detail Sheets is required, the new detail is produced on A4 size tracing paper using a standard format. This enables it to be added to the original collection and to be easily re-used.

The standard format is illustrated in Figure 6

The detail reference number is in two parts, the first part indicating the functional group, the second part the actual detail.

New details are assigned a reference number by the use of the appropriate functional group number and a detail number which follows consecutively from the last detail filed in that group.

The title of the new detail is then added to the contents list prefacing each section.

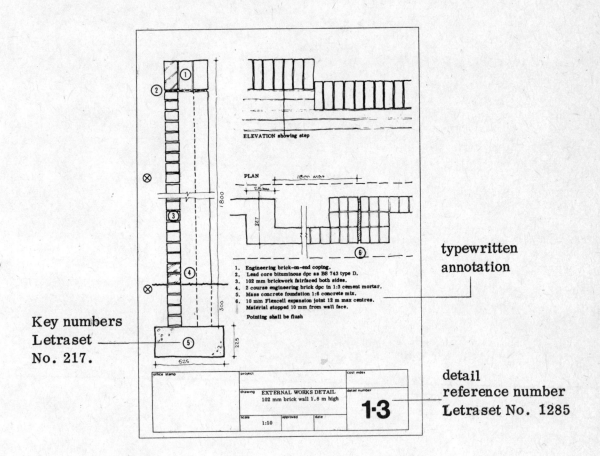

FIGURE 6   Layout of Standard Sheet

1.0   FREESTANDING WALLS

Choice of Bricks and Blocks

Bricks used in freestanding external walls, being exposed on both sides, are more prone to deterioration through frost action than the same bricks used, for example, in the external wall of a building.

Frost resistant bricks are generally those with low water absorbencies. However, certain types of stock bricks with absorbencies of up to 20% are frost resistant because their highly porous structure allows ice to expand within the brick without causing damage.

British Standard 3921 : 1974 defines three qualities of clay brick; internal ordinary and special.

' Ordinary ' quality bricks are not required to be frost resistant.

' Special ' quality bricks are required to be resistant to frost.   Evidence of frost resistance is required from the manufacturer in the form of a satisfactory 3 year weathering test either in a building or in a sample panel. In the absence of experimental evidence, a brick with strength greater than 48.5 N/mm^2 or a water absorption less than 7% is deemed to be frost resistant.

External free standing brick walls are also subject to deterioration following the reaction of soluble sulphates present in the bricks with the tricalcium aluminate constituent in ordinary Portland cement.   The reaction is accompanied by expansion of the mortar and subsequent cracking.

Sulphate attack can be avoided by the use of a 'special' quality brick as defined by B.S. 3921 : 1974.   The B.S. limits the soluble salt content of bricks of 'special' quality but not those of 'ordinary' quality.   Alternatively, use a richer mortar mix, e.g. 1 : 3 or a sulphate resisting cement.

Concrete blocks used in freestanding external walls should be Type A, as defined in B.S. 2028, 1364 : 1968.   A rough surface texture helps reduce weather staining.   Special pierced concrete blocks are also available. Calcium silicate bricks should be class 3 or higher as defined in B.S. 187.

Foundations

The depth and width of a foundation will vary according to the type of subsoil. On average subsoils a depth of 450 - 600 mm is usually sufficient; on shrinkable clay the depth may have to be 900 mm or greater.   A maximum width of 525 mm for unreinforced concrete foundations for 225 mm wide walls is advised.

A concrete mix of 1 : 6 is used in all the details although other mixes may be equally suitable.

Foundations can be omitted altogether where a wall is below 500 mm in height. The top soil should be removed and the brickwork built off the top of the subsoil which should be thoroughly compacted. Where more than 150 mm of topsoil has to be removed, the level of the excavation can be made up with well consolidated clinker.

Mortar

In a sulphate-free situation use a relatively weak mortar, e.g. 1 : 1 : 6, with clay bricks. If sulphates are present in the bricks a sulphate resisting cement or a stronger mix should be used, as recommended under 'Choice of Brick'. Calcium silicate bricks are generally laid in a weaker gauge than clay bricks. Brickwork below ground level and up to 150 mm above ground level, should be laid in a 1 : 3 cement mortar mix.

Expansion Joints

Expansion joints are necessary to accommodate thermal and moisture expansion. A 10 mm joint should be provided every 12 m for clay bricks and concrete blocks and every 6 m for calcium silicate (sand lime) bricks. Copings should not cross expansion joints.

Damp proof courses

A damp proof course is required 150 mm from ground level. This should preferably be 2 course of engineering bricks with a maximum absorbency of 4.5% laid in 1 : 3 mortar. An alternative is 2 courses of 5 mm natural slate laid in 1 : 3 mortar, breaking joints.

Polythene or other flexible sheet material should not be used in this situation as the break in tensile bond between the brick and mortar will result in failure of the wall at this point when subjected to wind pressure.

A damp proof course is also necessary at the top of the wall under the coping if the coping is a porous material such as brick on edge. If the coping is an impermeable material such as metal, PVC or engineering bricks, no damp proof course is required.

Although natural slate or clay tile is the best damp proof course in this position, a lead core bituminous damp proof course can also be used.

If a damp and mossy appearance to the lower parts of a wall is not objected to the dpc may be omitted provided that the bricks are of 'special' quality and a strong mortar mix (e.g. 1 : 3) is used. The same applies to the dpc under the coping.

Copings

The purpose of the coping is first, to prevent water seepage into the wall from the top and second, to shed water clear of the wall. The usual practice of using a brick on edge coping is acceptable because it is the damp proof course under the coping that is functioning as a coping and not the brick on edge.

Because of the presence of the damp proof course, brick on edge copings tend to become saturated and are particularly susceptible to frost damage and movement.

End bricks of brick copings should be held in position by metal cramps. Cramps can also be built into the top of the wall at a spacing of 900 mm to secure the coping bricks along the length of the wall.

Design

The stability of free-standing walls can be improved by adding piers, staggering the wall in bays or increasing the thickness of the wall.

The thickness of a free standing wall can be estimated using the following table.

Wind Pressure		Height to Thickness Ratio
N/m^2	lb/ft^2	
285	6 (very sheltered)	10
575	12 (sheltered)	7
860	18 (normal)	5
1150	24 (exposed)	4

All walls over 1.8 m high should be referred to a structural engineer for checking. Stability calculations may also be required by the district surveyor of building inspector for such walls.

REFERENCES

Brick Development Association
  The Design of Freestanding Brick Walls   July 1972
  Mortars for Brickwork   Sept 1973

Building Research Establishment
  Digests Nos. 65 and 66
  The selection of Clay Building Bricks
  Digest No. 89
  Sulphate Attack on Brickwork
  Digest No. 77
  Damp Proof Courses

British Standards Institute
 BS 3921 : 1974
 Specification for Clay Bricks and Blocks
 BS 2028, 1364 : 1968
 Pre-cast Concrete Blocks
 Cp 121 Part 1
 Brick and Block Masonry

Cement and Concrete Association
 Concrete Block Walls 1966
 Screen Walls of Pierced Concrete Walls

Architectural Press London
 M. Gage and T. Kirkbride
 Design in Blockwork 2nd Edition 1976
 C. C. Handisyde
 Hard Landscape in Brick Chapter 11, 1976

NBA + 'Building' Commodity File
 Concrete Blocks
 Materials F Section 01
 Bricks
 Materials F Section 02

1.0   FREE STANDING WALLS

1.1   215 mm brick wall 1.8 m high
1.2   215 mm brick wall 925 mm high
1.3   102 mm brick wall 1.8 m high
1.4   102 mm brick wall 900 mm high
1.5   215 mm brick wall 940 mm high
1.6   Dwarf brick wall
1.7   Perforated brickwork screen
1.8   Decorative concrete block screen
1.9   225 mm brick wall rat-trap band 1.8 m high
1.10   Concrete block wall 1.8 m high
1.11   Concrete block wall 900 mm high

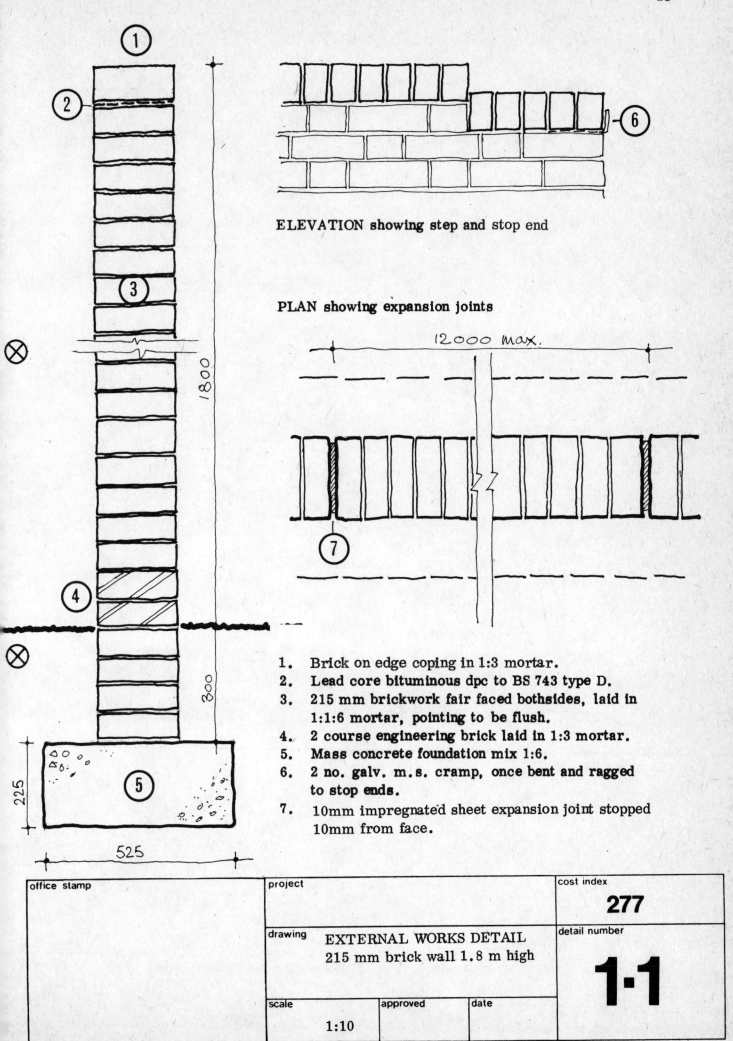

ELEVATION showing step and stop end

PLAN showing expansion joints

12000 MAX.

1. Brick on edge coping in 1:3 mortar.
2. Lead core bituminous dpc to BS 743 type D.
3. 215 mm brickwork fair faced bothsides, laid in 1:1:6 mortar, pointing to be flush.
4. 2 course engineering brick laid in 1:3 mortar.
5. Mass concrete foundation mix 1:6.
6. 2 no. galv. m.s. cramp, once bent and ragged to stop ends.
7. 10mm impregnated sheet expansion joint stopped 10mm from face.

office stamp	project		cost index
			277
	drawing EXTERNAL WORKS DETAIL 215 mm brick wall 1.8 m high		detail number
			1·1
	scale 1:10	approved	date

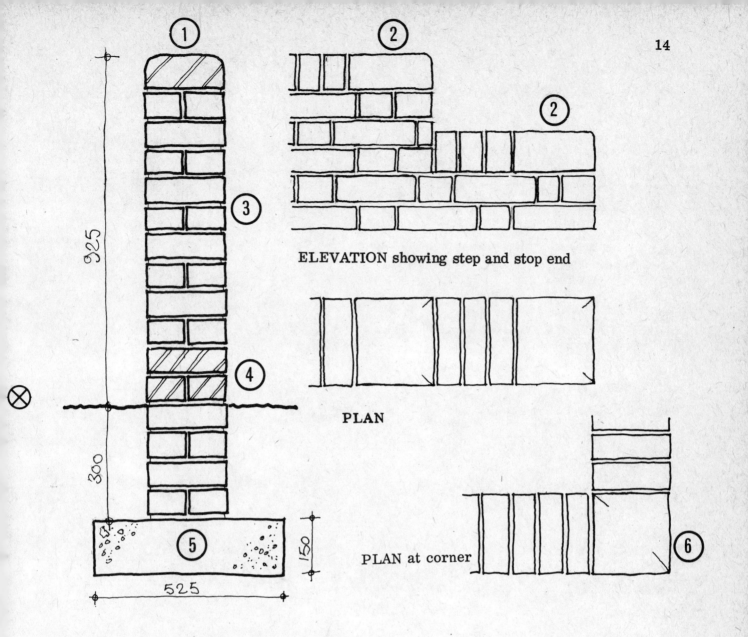

ELEVATION showing step and stop end

PLAN

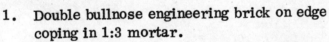

PLAN at corner

1. Double bullnose engineering brick on edge coping in 1:3 mortar.
2. 215 x 215 mm stop end to double bullnose coping.
3. 215 mm brickwork, flemish bond, set in 1:1:6 mortar flush pointing 10 mm expansion joint every 12 m.
4. 2 course engineering brick laid in 1:3 mortar.
5. Mass concrete foundation mix 1:6.
6. Bullnose external return on edge.

office stamp	project		cost index
			212
	drawing		detail number
	EXTERNAL WORKS DETAIL 215 mm brick wall 925 mm high		**1·2**
	scale	approved	date
	1:10		

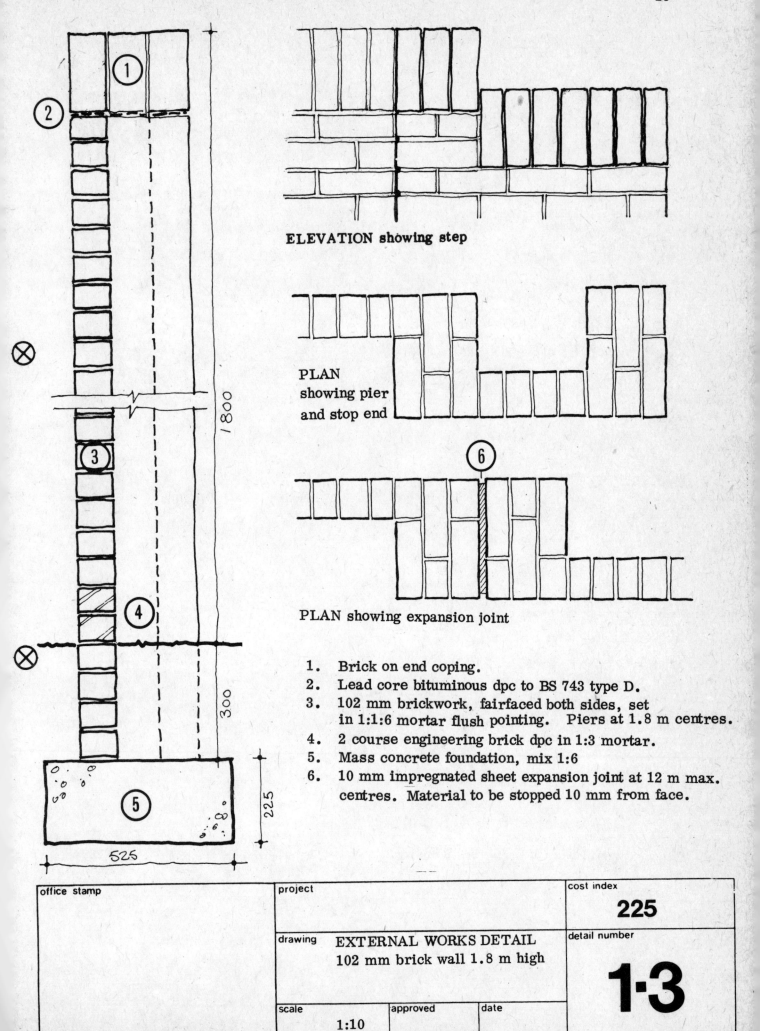

15

ELEVATION showing step

PLAN
showing pier
and stop end

PLAN showing expansion joint

1. Brick on end coping.
2. Lead core bituminous dpc to BS 743 type D.
3. 102 mm brickwork, fairfaced both sides, set
   in 1:1:6 mortar flush pointing. Piers at 1.8 m centres.
4. 2 course engineering brick dpc in 1:3 mortar.
5. Mass concrete foundation, mix 1:6
6. 10 mm impregnated sheet expansion joint at 12 m max.
   centres. Material to be stopped 10 mm from face.

office stamp	project		cost index
			225
	drawing EXTERNAL WORKS DETAIL 102 mm brick wall 1.8 m high		detail number
			1·3
	scale 1:10	approved	date

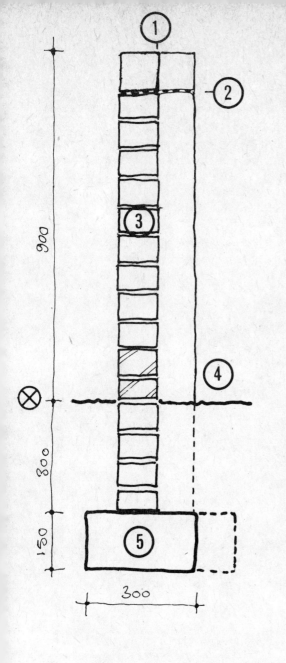

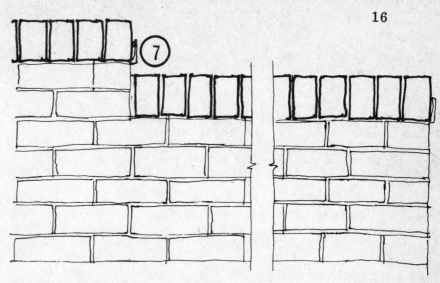

16

ELEVATION showing step and stop end

PLAN showing bonding of intermediate and end piers

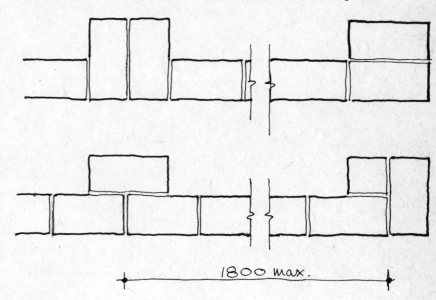

1800 max.

1. Half brick on edge
2. Lead core bituminous dpc to BS 743 type D
3. 102 mm brick wall fairfaced both sides laid in 1:1:6 mortar, flush pointing.
4. 2 course engineering brick dpc
5. Mass concrete foundation concrete mix 1:6
6. Expansion joint at pier at 12 m max. centres. Joint filled with impregnated sheet material stopped 10 mm from wall face.
7. 2 no. galv. m.s. cramp, once bent and ragged to stop ends.

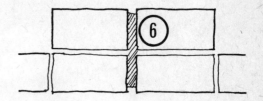

PLAN at expansion joint

office stamp	project		cost index
			142
	drawing	EXTERNAL WORKS DETAIL 102 mm brick wall 900 mm high	detail number
			1·4
	scale 1:10	approved	date

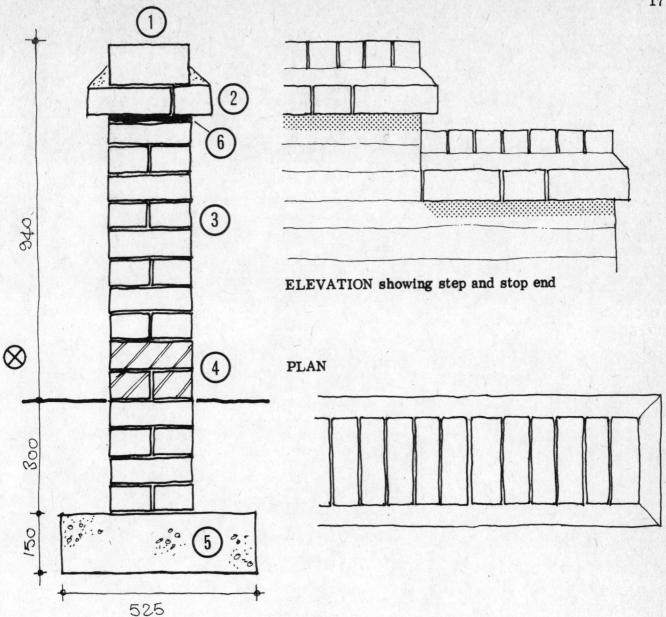

17

ELEVATION showing step and stop end

PLAN

1. Brick on edge coping in 1:3 mortar.
2. Oversailing course with 1:1:6 mortar fillet.
3. 215 mm brickwork, English bond, in 1:1:6 mortar. 10 mm expansion joint every 12 m. Expansion joint material to be impregnated sheet stopped 10 mm from face. Pointing to be flush.
4. 2 course engineering brick in 1:3 mortar.
5. Concrete footing. Concrete mix 1:6.
6. Lead core dpc as BS 743 Type D.

office stamp	project		cost index
			182
	drawing	**EXTERNAL WORKS DETAIL** 215 mm brick wall 940 mm high	detail number
	scale 1:10	approved	date

1·5

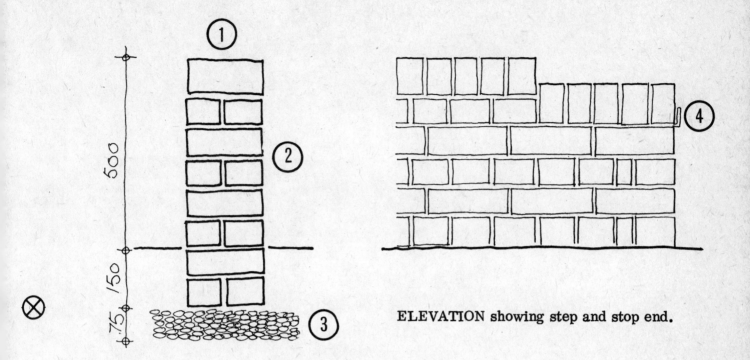

ELEVATION showing step and stop end.

1. Brick on edge coping.

2. 215 mm brickwork; flemish bond.
    1:1:6 cement mortar, flush pointing.

3. 75 mm well rammed and wetted clinker bed.

4. 2 no. galv. m.s. cramp, once bent and ragged to
    stop ends.

office stamp	project		cost index
			100
	drawing	EXTERNAL WORKS DETAIL Dwarf brick wall.	detail number
			1·6
	scale	approved	date
	1:10		

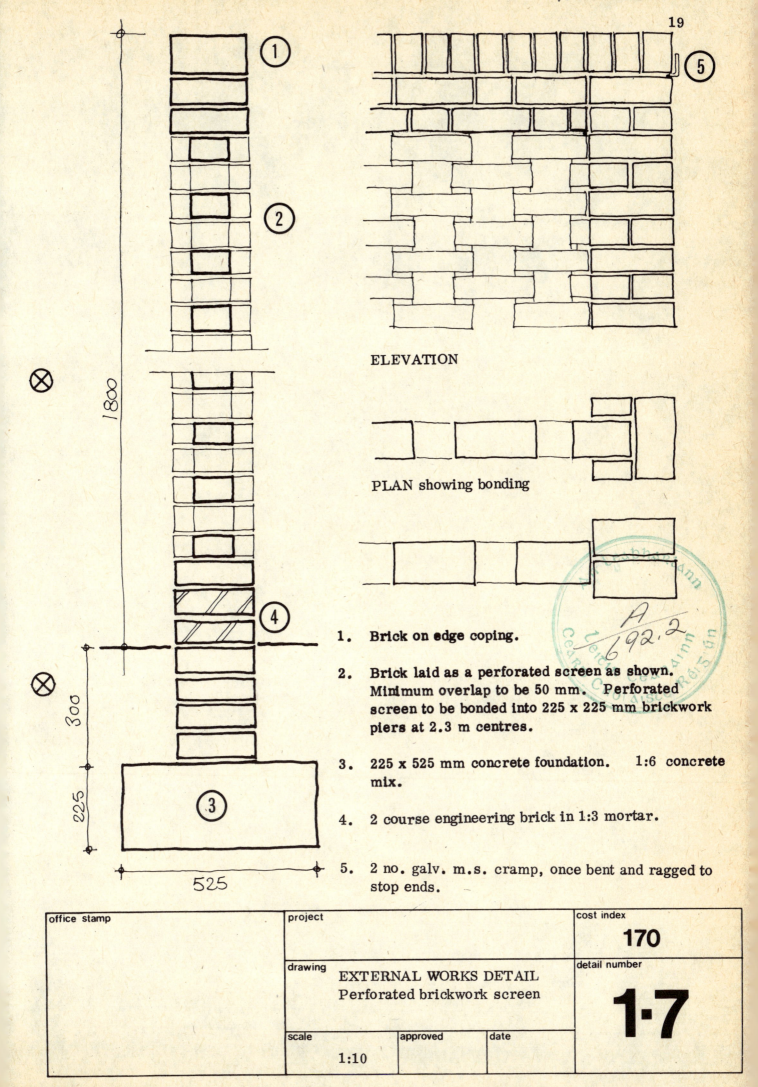

ELEVATION

PLAN showing bonding

1. Brick on edge coping.

2. Brick laid as a perforated screen as shown.
   Minimum overlap to be 50 mm. Perforated
   screen to be bonded into 225 x 225 mm brickwork
   piers at 2.3 m centres.

3. 225 x 525 mm concrete foundation.   1:6 concrete
   mix.

4. 2 course engineering brick in 1:3 mortar.

5. 2 no. galv. m.s. cramp, once bent and ragged to
   stop ends.

office stamp	project		cost index
			170
	drawing		detail number
	EXTERNAL WORKS DETAIL		
	Perforated brickwork screen		**1·7**
	scale	approved	date	
	1:10			

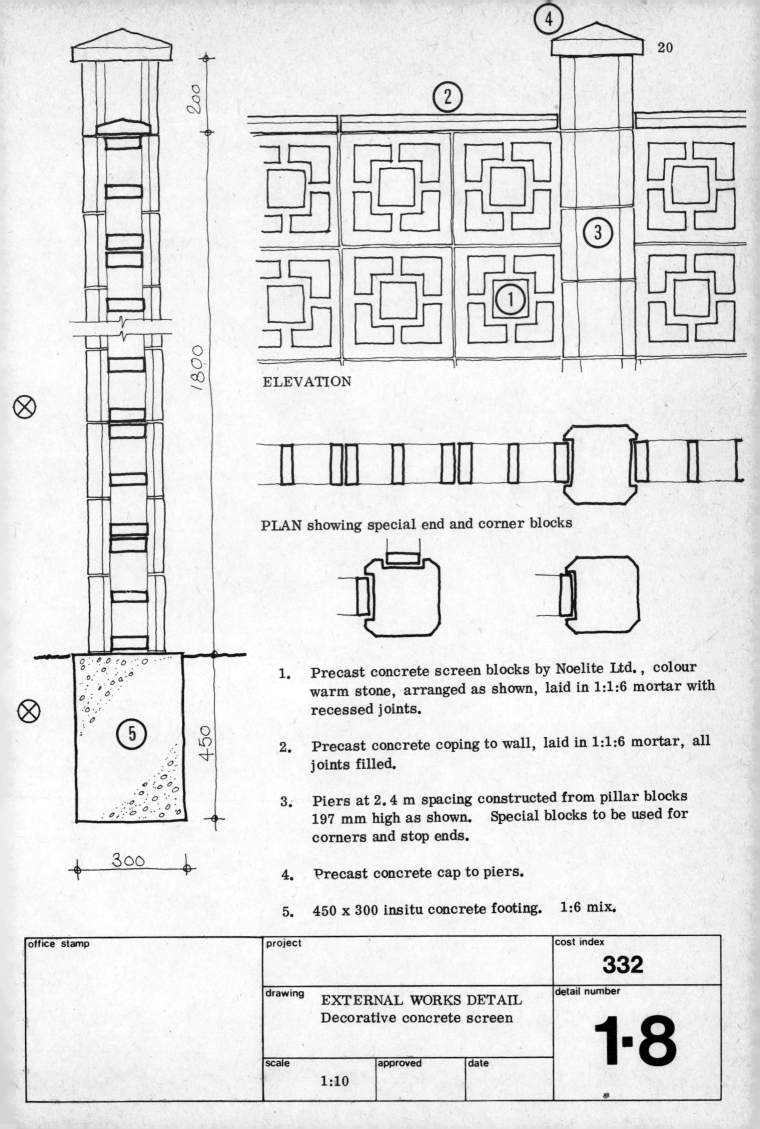

ELEVATION

PLAN showing special end and corner blocks

1. Precast concrete screen blocks by Noelite Ltd., colour warm stone, arranged as shown, laid in 1:1:6 mortar with recessed joints.

2. Precast concrete coping to wall, laid in 1:1:6 mortar, all joints filled.

3. Piers at 2.4 m spacing constructed from pillar blocks 197 mm high as shown. Special blocks to be used for corners and stop ends.

4. Precast concrete cap to piers.

5. 450 x 300 insitu concrete footing. 1:6 mix.

office stamp	project		cost index
			332
	drawing		detail number
	EXTERNAL WORKS DETAIL		
	Decorative concrete screen		**1·8**
	scale	approved	date
	1:10		

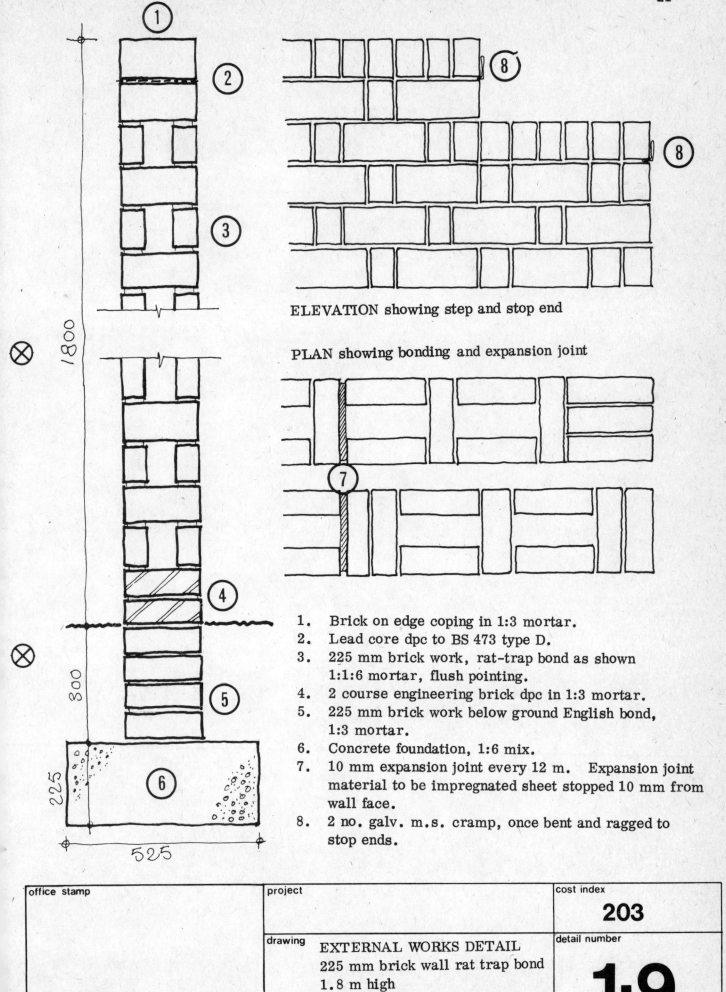

21

ELEVATION showing step and stop end

PLAN showing bonding and expansion joint

1. Brick on edge coping in 1:3 mortar.
2. Lead core dpc to BS 473 type D.
3. 225 mm brick work, rat-trap bond as shown
   1:1:6 mortar, flush pointing.
4. 2 course engineering brick dpc in 1:3 mortar.
5. 225 mm brick work below ground English bond,
   1:3 mortar.
6. Concrete foundation, 1:6 mix.
7. 10 mm expansion joint every 12 m. Expansion joint
   material to be impregnated sheet stopped 10 mm from
   wall face.
8. 2 no. galv. m.s. cramp, once bent and ragged to
   stop ends.

office stamp	project		cost index
			203
	drawing EXTERNAL WORKS DETAIL 225 mm brick wall rat trap bond 1.8 m high		detail number
			1·9
	scale 1:10	approved	date

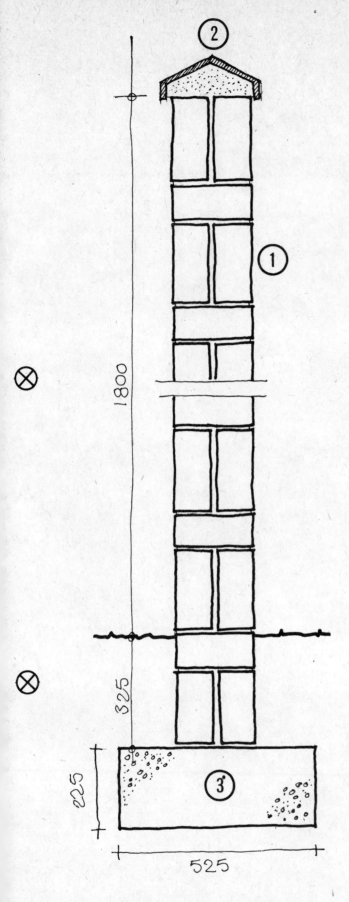

22

1800

525

225

525

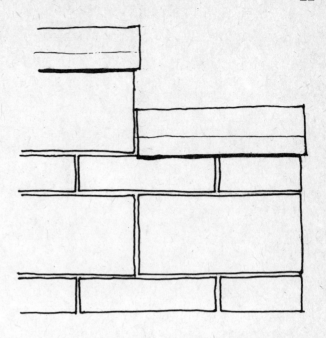

ELEVATION showing step and stop end

1. 100 x 225 x 450 mm dense concrete blocks to BS 2028 Type A with plain face and edges. Alternate courses to be laid flat as shown. 1:1:6 mortar, flush pointing. Paint finish as specified. 10 mm expansion joint every 12 m. Expansion joint material stopped 10 mm from face.

2. Clay angle ridge tile on 1:3 mortar bed, joints to be mortar pointed.

3. Mass concrete foundation 1:6 mix.

office stamp	project		cost index
			112
	drawing		detail number
	EXTERNAL WORKS DETAIL Concrete block wall 1.8 m high		**1·10**
	scale	approved	date
	1:10		

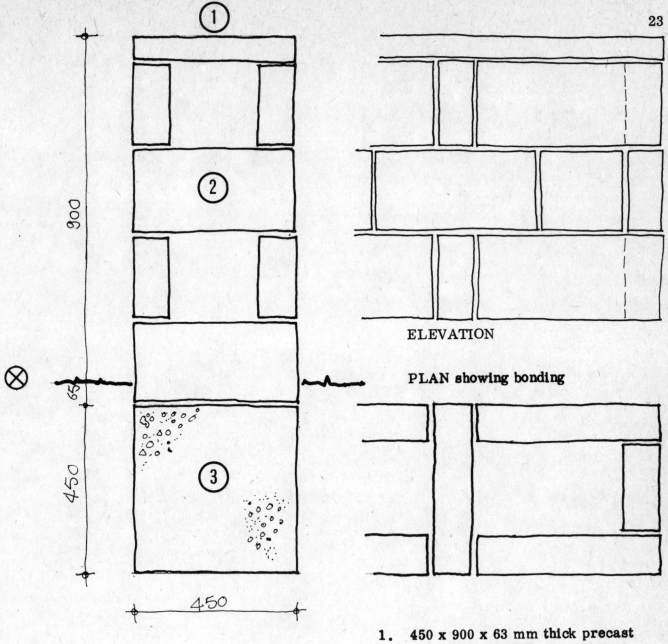

23

ELEVATION

PLAN showing bonding

1. 450 x 900 x 63 mm thick precast concrete paving flag as coping.

2. 100 x 450 x 225 dense concrete blocks to BS 2028 Type A, with plain edges and faces, laid rat trap bond as shown. Paint finish as specified.

3. Mass concrete foundation 1:6 mix.

office stamp	project		cost index
			106
	drawing EXTERNAL WORKS DETAIL Concrete block wall 900 mm high		detail number
	scale 1:10	approved	date	**1·11**

2.0   RETAINING STRUCTURES

a). Brickwork Retaining Walls

Choice of Brick

The remarks made in section 1.0 "Freestanding Walls" apply equally to brick retaining walls.   In addition brick retaining walls should be protected from water percolation and sulphates in the retained soil by the use of an impervious backing to the retaining wall.   The backing can be asphalt tanking or cement render treated with a waterproofer.

Design

The following table can be used for the design of brick retaining walls up to 1800 mm high:

Height from Ground level	Thickness	Width of Foundation 110 kN/m^2 55 kN/m^2 min. bearing pressures		Thickness of Foundation
900	215	525	525	225
1200	327.5	600	600	225
1500	440	675	900	225
1800	552.5	750	1050	225

Drainage

Back fill should be sulphate-free granular material.   37 mm diameter weepholes should be provided at 3 m centres.   Weepholes should discharge at least 150 mm above ground level.   A 100 mm land drain should be laid below the level of the weep holes.

Expansion Joints

10 mm expansion joints should be provided at 5 m centres.   Expansion joints should be protected from water seepage with a 225 mm wide vertical damp proof course.

Damp Proof Course

A damp proof course of 2 courses of engineering bricks laid in 1 : 3 mortar must be used with retaining walls.   Flexible sheet materials should not be used.

b). <u>Concrete Retaining Walls</u>

Concrete retaining walls are either cast in situ or pre-cast.

In situ reinforced concrete retaining walls should generally be designed by a structural engineer.   Brickwork facings can be tied to concrete walls by the use of butterfly wire ties or dove tail anchor slots.

Pre-cast concrete retaining wall units are available either as an L shaped unit or as small units which are interlocked to form a lattice 'crib' then filled with topsoil and established by planting.

c). <u>Timber Retaining Walls</u>

Little design guidance exists on this subject.

Timber species must be durable such as larch, sweet chestnut or oak. Softwood when used must be pressure impregnated with preservative by a vacuum process.

Timber thickness should be a minimum of 100 mm, preferably 150 mm.

Depth of insertion should at least equal the height of the retained earth.

REFERENCES

Brick Development Association
  The Design of Freestanding Brick Walls July 1972

The Architectural Press London
  M. Gage and M. Vandenberg
  Hard Landscape in Concrete p.99 1975

27

2.0   RETAINING STRUCTURES

2.1   Brick retaining wall 900 mm high
2.2   Brick retaining wall 2.1 m high
2.3   Pre-cast concrete retaining wall 600 mm high
2.4   Timber retaining wall
2.5   Concrete flag retaining wall

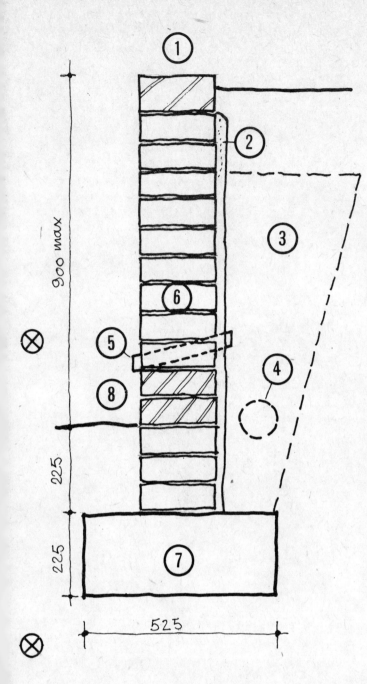

900 max

225

225

525

1. Engineering brick-on-edge coping

2. 1:3 waterproofed cement/sand render

3. Sulphate free hardcore back filling consolidated as specified.

4. 100 mm clay ware drain laid butt jointed.

5. 37 mm black pvc weep pipe 3.0 m centres.

6. 215 mm brickwork 1:3 cement mortar

7. Concrete foundation 1:6 mix.

8. 2 course engineering brick dpc laid in 1:3 mortar.

office stamp	project	cost index
		155
	drawing EXTERNAL WORKS DETAIL Brick retaining wall 900 mm high	detail number
		2·1
	scale 1:10 approved date	

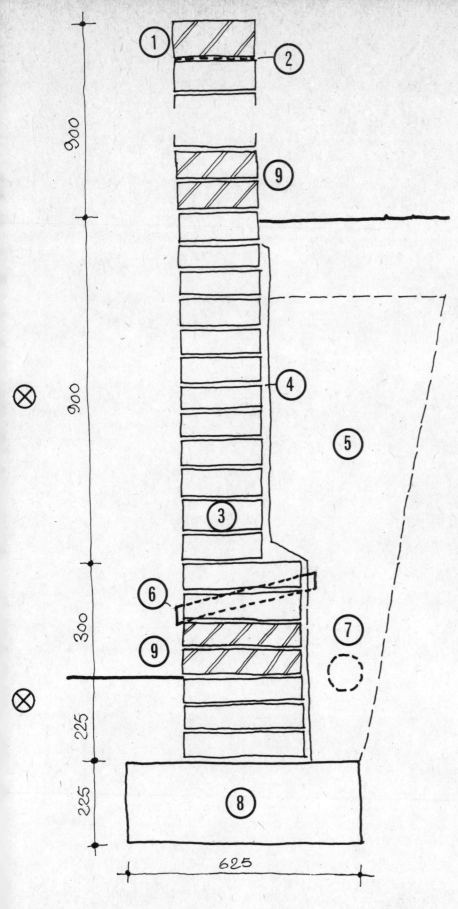

29

1. Engineering brick on edge.

2. Lead core bituminous felt dpc to BS 743 type D.

3. 215 mm brickwork in 1:3 cement mortar.

4. 1:3 waterproofed cement/sand render.

5. Sulphate free hardcore backfill consolidated as specified.

6. 37 mm black pvc weep pipe 3.0 m centres.

7. 100 mm clayware drain laid butt jointed.

8. Concrete foundation 1:6 mix.

9. 2 course engineering brick dpc laid in 1:3 mortar

office stamp	project		cost index
			276
	drawing	EXTERNAL WORKS DETAIL Brick retaining wall 2.1 m high	detail number
			2·2
	scale 1:10	approved	date

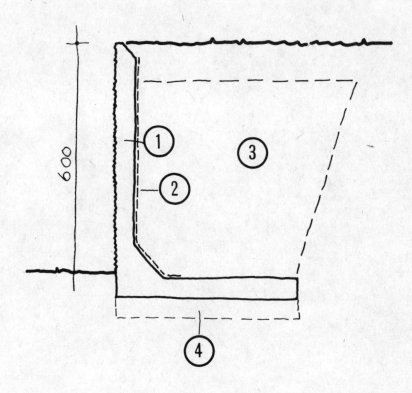

1. 'Mono wall' pre-cast concrete retaining wall type 2, by Mono Concrete Ltd., laid with 10 mm open joints and mitred joints at external corners. Exposed aggregate facing to be No. 385, black granite.

2. 1000 g. polythene membrane lapped 100 mm at joints.

3. Consolidated backfill as specified.

4. 50 mm sand bed.

office stamp	project		cost index
			201
	drawing EXTERNAL WORKS DETAIL Pre-cast concrete retaining wall 600 mm high		detail number
			2·3
	scale	approved	date
	1:10		

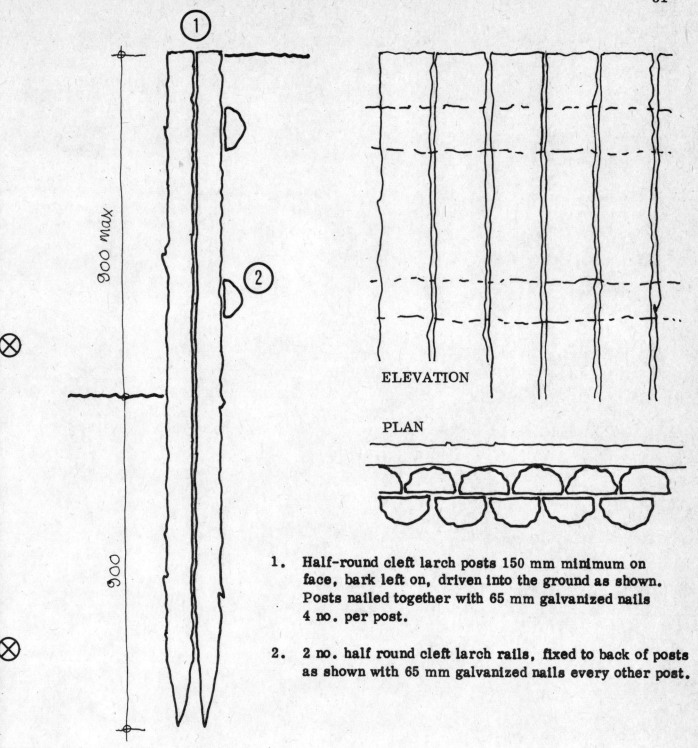

31

ELEVATION

PLAN

1. Half-round cleft larch posts 150 mm minimum on face, bark left on, driven into the ground as shown. Posts nailed together with 65 mm galvanized nails 4 no. per post.

2. 2 no. half round cleft larch rails, fixed to back of posts as shown with 65 mm galvanized nails every other post.

office stamp	project		cost index
			152
	drawing	EXTERNAL WORKS DETAIL	detail number
		Timber retaining wall	
	scale	approved	date	**2·4**
	1:10			

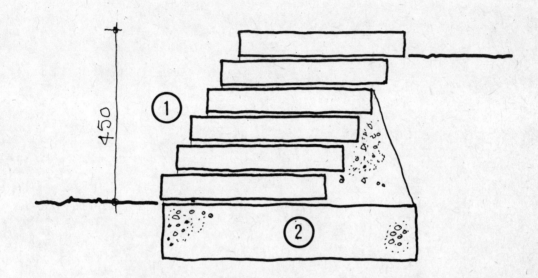

32

1. Wall constructed of 450 x 900 mm x 63 mm thick precast concrete paving flags, set on cement mortar bed and each course set back 25 mm from face as shown.

2. 150 mm concrete foundation and backing. 1:2:4 concrete mix.

office stamp	project		cost index 100
	drawing EXTERNAL WORKS DETAIL Concrete flag wall		detail number 2·5
	scale 1:10	approved	date

3.0   FENCES

a). Timber Fences

Timber Type and Preservation

The most common fencing timbers are oak, sweet chestnut and cedar. These need no preservation for above ground situations. Where these timbers are used as posts, the ends should be impregnated with creosote by immersion in a creosote bath maintained at 94°C for several hours and then allowed to cool.

All softwood used in fencing shall be preservative impregnated by a vacuum process.

Timber Sizes

BS 1722, pt 5 can be used as a guide to timber sizes for fencing purposes.

Post Spacing

Posts should be spaced at 2.7 m maximum centres for morticed fencing and 1.8 m maximum centres for nailed fencing.

Depth of Insertion

Under normal exposure conditions a post insertion depth of 500 mm is sufficient for a 1.0 m high fence and 750 mm for a 1.8 m high fence. If a concrete surround is used these can be reduced to 400 mm and 657 mm respectively because of the greater face area given by the concrete.

The advantages of using a concrete surround to the posts are not clear-cut. Although a shallower depth of insertion is required, rotting of posts is sometimes accelerated because of ground water accumulating on top of the concrete. In addition replacement of posts is made more difficult because of the presence of the concrete in the ground. The best advice seems to be to use a concrete surround in loose or made up ground and where concrete is available, for example, on a building site. Where concrete is not available, for example, in forest or farm fencing and the ground is virgin the post should be set in an augered hole and back filled with hard consolidated excavated material.

Fixings

All fixings used for fencing should be galvanised. Drive screws or wood screws should be used for fixing in public areas. Where bolts are used the nuts should be recessed into the post or the projecting threads burred over.

35

Finish

Suitable timbers such as, oak, cedar, sweet chestnut or larch can be left unfinished.   Otherwise use a two coat application of wood dye or a coloured preservative.   Some brush applied preservatives are not compatible with vacuum preservation processes which include water repellants.

Opaque oil paint systems can be used satisfactorily on timber which has been vacuum impregnated with a preservative which does not include a water repellant.   Where a water repellant has been used loss of adhesion of the paint film may result unless a special primer is used.   In this situation the paint manufacturer should be consulted.

Changes in Level

Changes in level are accommodated when using fences made from prefabricated panels by stepping each panel.   Posts at the steps will have to be increased in length.

Where post and rail fencing is used, changes in level are accommodated by inclining the rails in the mortices, while keeping the posts vertical.

b). ## Metal Fencing

Sizes of Members

The materials used almost exclusively for metal fencing are wrought iron amd mild steel.   BS 1722, pt 8 and 9 can be used as a guide for sizes and spacing of members.

Space between vertical members should not be less than 100 mm or more than 120 mm.

Standards

An insertion depth of 600 mm is suitable for a fence up to 1.8 m high. Spacing should be 2.7 m max.   A wing plate parallel to the fence line should be welded to each standard.   Standards should have a bearing plate welded to the base.

Standards for fences incorporating strained wire should have stays fixed at 60° to horizontal at corners and ends.

Because of small face dimension of metal members, a concrete surround to the standard should always be used.

36

Preservation and Finish

BS 1722, pt 8 specifies a range of ex-works finishes, the usual finish being a red-oxide primer or hot-dip galvanising after fabrication.

The finish coating shall be paint applied as two undercoats and one gloss top coat.

Changes in Level

Prefabricated metal fencing is accommodated to changes in level by stepping the panels or fabricating special inclined panels.   With either method, the profile of the ground must be known in advance of fabrication.

REFERENCES

British Standards Institute
  BS 1722 Fences
  Parts 1 - 11

E and F. N. Spon Ltd.
  Spon's Landscape Handbook

Monmouthshire County Council
  Fences in the Countryside 1974

Central Electricity Generating Board
  Design Memorandum on the Use of Fences

Greater London Council
  Development and Materials Bulletin No. 79 Oct/Nov 1974
  Use of Pigmented Water Repellant Finishes for External
  Softwood Joinery - A. Warning

Forestry Commission
  Forest Fencing

NBA + 'Building' Commodity File
  Components (90) Section 02
  Fencing

3.0   FENCES

3.1   Close board fence 1.8 m high
3.2   Close board fence 1.0 m high
3.3   Woven wood fence 1.8 m high
3.4   Waney edge over lap fence with trellis top
3.5   Osier hurdles 1.8 m high
3.6   Double sided timber palisade fence 1.8 m high
3.7   Timber post and rail fence
3.8   Timber palisade fence 1050 mm high
3.9   Diagonal boarding fence
3.10   Timber and PVC palisade fence
3.11   Timber palisade fence 1.8 m high
3.12   Chain link fence 1.8 m high
3.13   Lincolnshire post and rail fence
3.14   Cleft chestnut fence 1.0 m high
3.15   Cleft chestnut and wire fence 1050 mm high
3.16   Timber and plastic mesh fence 875 mm high
3.17   Two rail Sussex fence 900 mm high
3.18   Bow topped steel fence 900 mm high
3.19   Vertical bar steel fence 1050 mm high

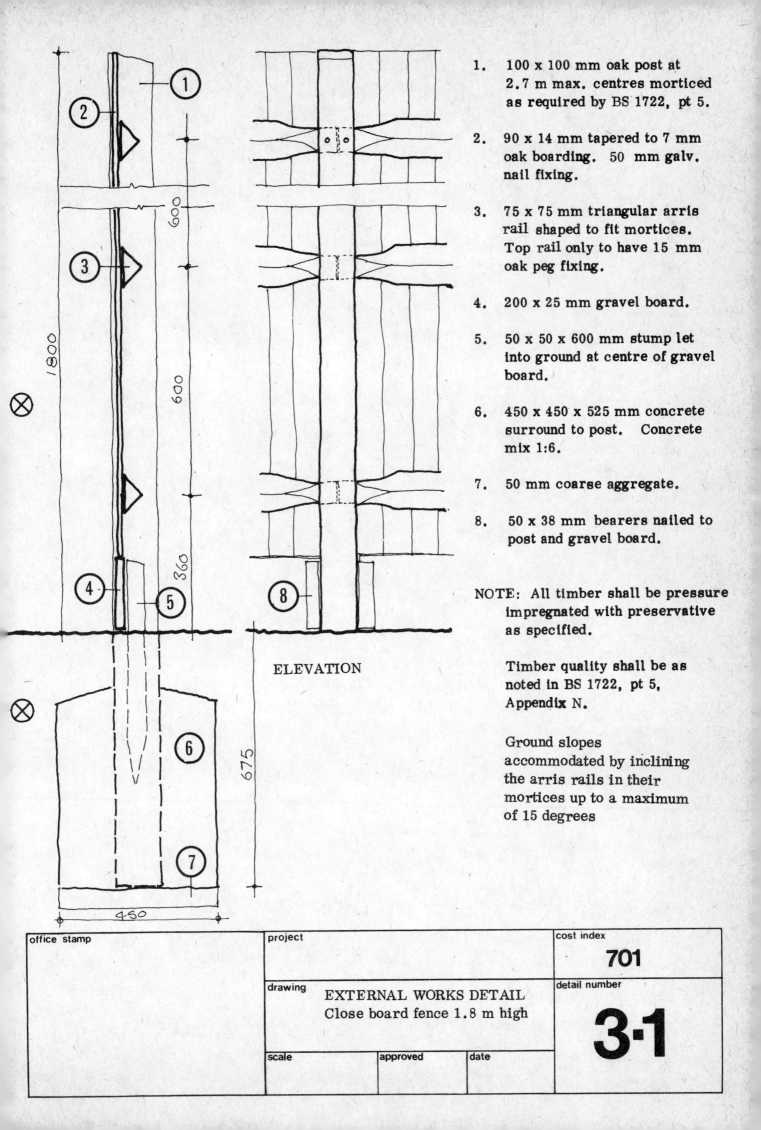

ELEVATION

1. 100 x 100 mm oak post at 2.7 m max. centres morticed as required by BS 1722, pt 5.

2. 90 x 14 mm tapered to 7 mm oak boarding. 50 mm galv. nail fixing.

3. 75 x 75 mm triangular arris rail shaped to fit mortices. Top rail only to have 15 mm oak peg fixing.

4. 200 x 25 mm gravel board.

5. 50 x 50 x 600 mm stump let into ground at centre of gravel board.

6. 450 x 450 x 525 mm concrete surround to post. Concrete mix 1:6.

7. 50 mm coarse aggregate.

8. 50 x 38 mm bearers nailed to post and gravel board.

NOTE: All timber shall be pressure impregnated with preservative as specified.

Timber quality shall be as noted in BS 1722, pt 5, Appendix N.

Ground slopes accommodated by inclining the arris rails in their mortices up to a maximum of 15 degrees

office stamp	project		cost index
			701
	drawing	EXTERNAL WORKS DETAIL Close board fence 1.8 m high	detail number
			3·1
	scale	approved	date

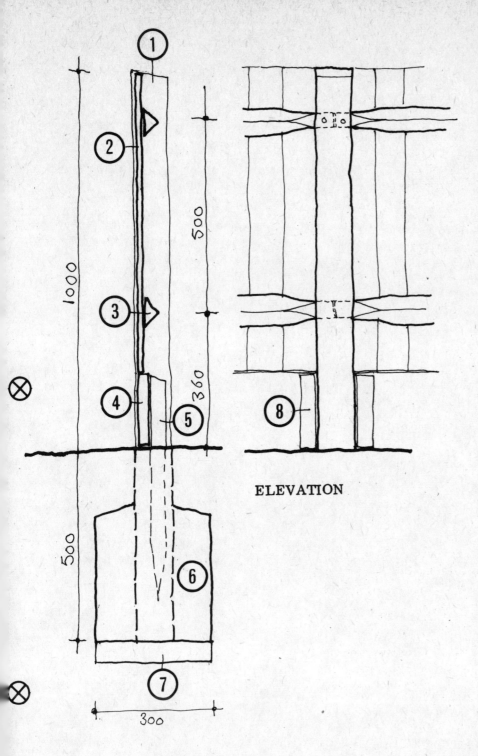

39

ELEVATION

1. 100 x 100 mm oak post at 2.7 m max. centres morticed as required by BS 1722 Pt 5.

2. 90 x 14 mm tapered to 7 mm oak boarding 50 mm galv. nail fixing.

3. 75 x 75 mm triangular arris rail shaped to fit mortises. Top rail only to have 15 mm timber peg fixing.

4. 200 x 25 mm gravel board

5. 50 x 50 x 600 mm stump let into ground at centre of gravel board.

6. 300 x 300 x 350 mm concrete surround to post. Concrete mix 1:6.

7. 50 mm coarse aggregate.

8. 50 x 38 m bearer nailed to post and gravel board.

NOTE: All timber shall be pressure impregnated with preservative as specified.

Timber quality shall be as noted in BS 1722 Pt 5, Appendix N.

Ground slopes accommodated by inclining the arris rails in their mortices up to a maximum of 15 degrees

office stamp	project		cost index
			416
	drawing EXTERNAL WORKS DETAIL Close board fence 1.0 m high		detail number
			3·2
	scale 1:10	approved	date

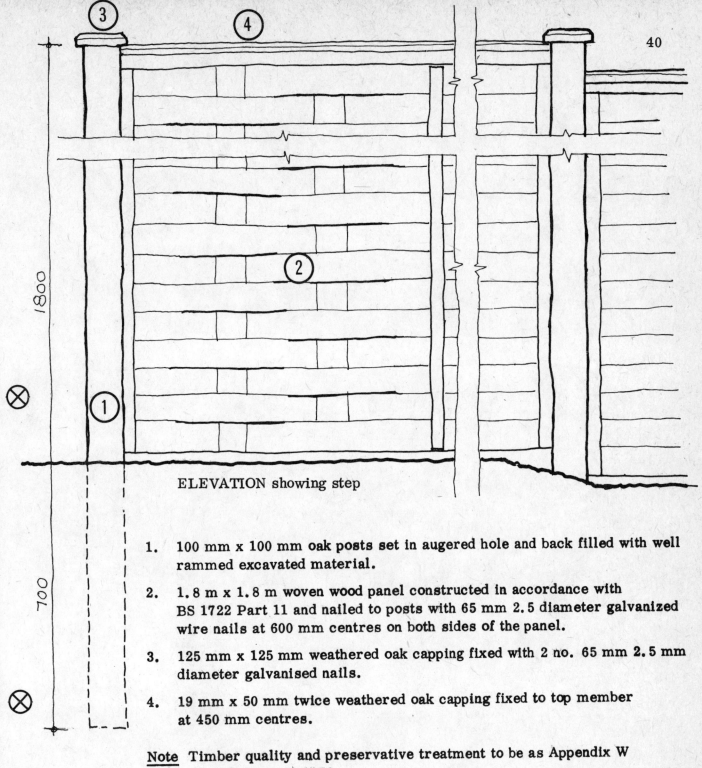

40

ELEVATION showing step

1. 100 mm x 100 mm oak posts set in augered hole and back filled with well rammed excavated material.

2. 1.8 m x 1.8 m woven wood panel constructed in accordance with BS 1722 Part 11 and nailed to posts with 65 mm 2.5 diameter galvanized wire nails at 600 mm centres on both sides of the panel.

3. 125 mm x 125 mm weathered oak capping fixed with 2 no. 65 mm 2.5 mm diameter galvanised nails.

4. 19 mm x 50 mm twice weathered oak capping fixed to top member at 450 mm centres.

Note Timber quality and preservative treatment to be as Appendix W BS 1722 Part 11 1972.

PLAN

office stamp	project		cost index
			468
	drawing	EXTERNAL WORKS DETAIL Woven wood fence 1.8 m high	detail number
			3·3
	scale 1:10	approved	date

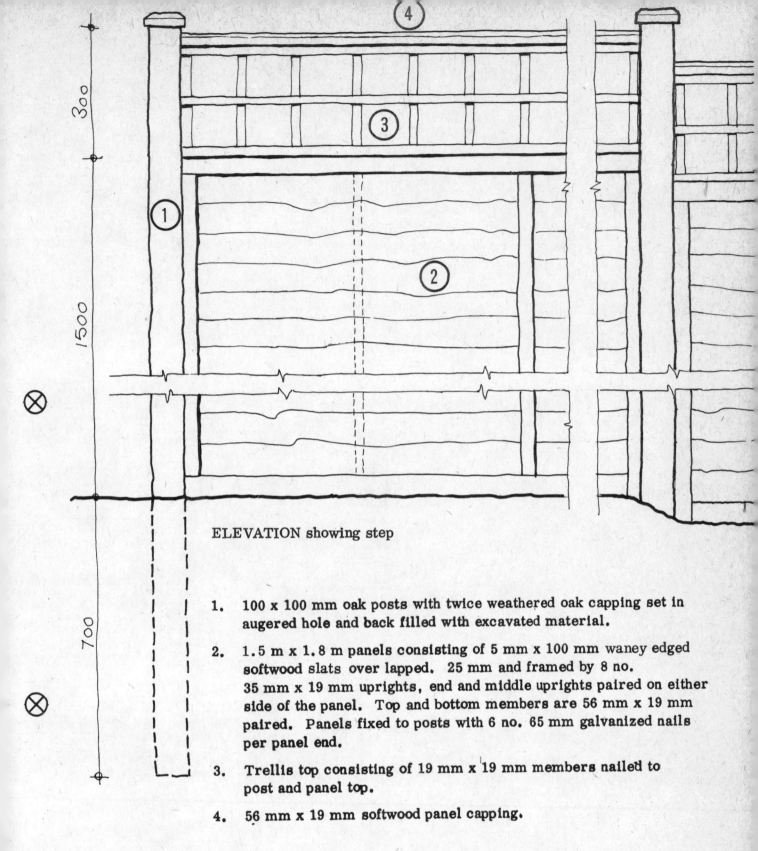

300

1500

700

ELEVATION showing step

1.   100 x 100 mm oak posts with twice weathered oak capping set in augered hole and back filled with excavated material.

2.   1.5 m x 1.8 m panels consisting of 5 mm x 100 mm waney edged softwood slats over lapped. 25 mm and framed by 8 no. 35 mm x 19 mm uprights, end and middle uprights paired on either side of the panel. Top and bottom members are 56 mm x 19 mm paired. Panels fixed to posts with 6 no. 65 mm galvanized nails per panel end.

3.   Trellis top consisting of 19 mm x 19 mm members nailed to post and panel top.

4.   56 mm x 19 mm softwood panel capping.

<u>Note</u> All timber to be pressure impregnated with preservative as specified. Finish to be two coats wood dye as specified.

office stamp	project		cost index
			494
	drawing EXTERNAL WORKS DETAIL Waney edge overlap board fence with trellis top		detail number
			3·4
	scale 1:10	approved date	

42

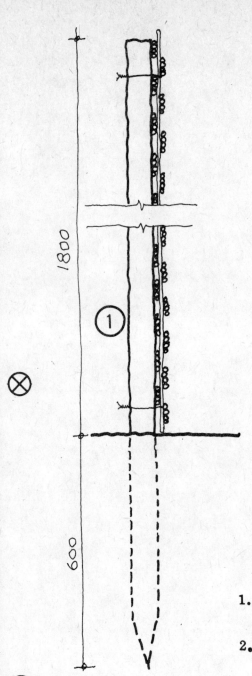

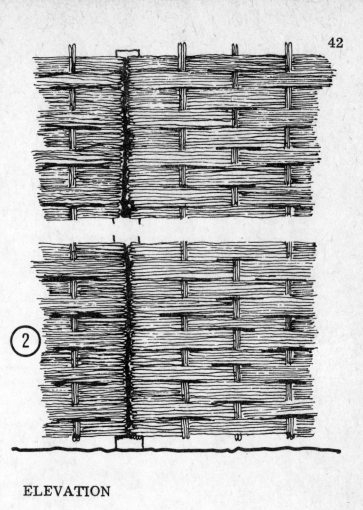

ELEVATION

1. Round softwood stakes, 75 mm diameter, preservative treated as specified, driven into the ground at 1.8 m centres.

2. Osier (willow) hurdles 1.8 m high x 1.8 m long, wired to stakes with 1.5 mm galvanized wire.

office stamp	project		cost index
			197
	drawing		detail number
	EXTERNAL WORKS DETAIL Osier hurdles 1.8 m high		
	scale	approved	date	**3·5**
	1:10			

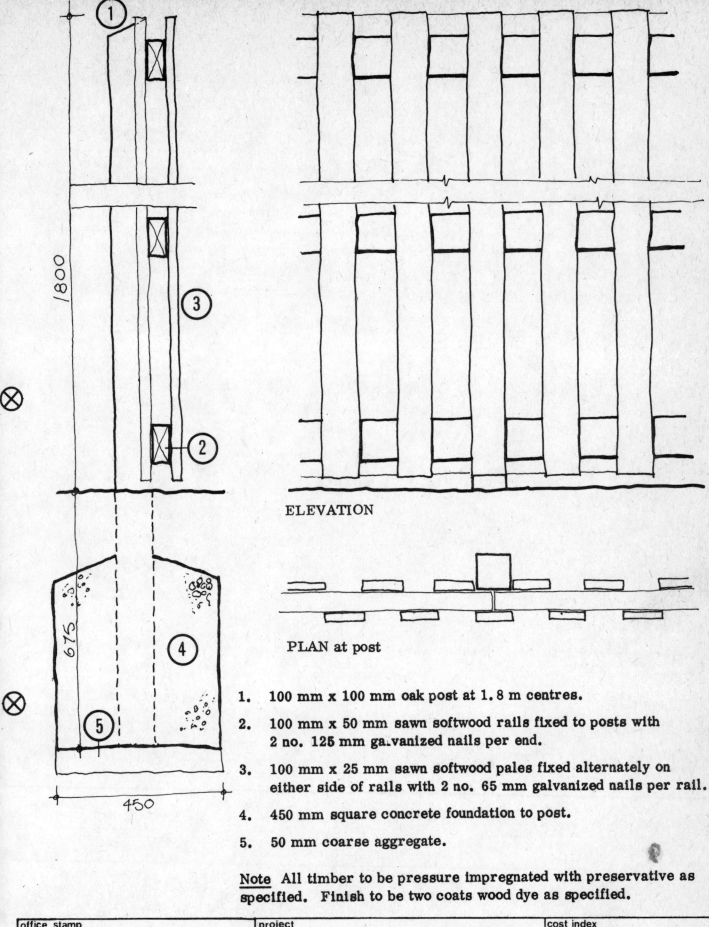

ELEVATION

PLAN at post

1. 100 mm x 100 mm oak post at 1.8 m centres.

2. 100 mm x 50 mm sawn softwood rails fixed to posts with 2 no. 125 mm galvanized nails per end.

3. 100 mm x 25 mm sawn softwood pales fixed alternately on either side of rails with 2 no. 65 mm galvanized nails per rail.

4. 450 mm square concrete foundation to post.

5. 50 mm coarse aggregate.

<u>Note</u> All timber to be pressure impregnated with preservative as specified. Finish to be two coats wood dye as specified.

office stamp	project		cost index
			633
	drawing EXTERNAL WORKS DETAIL Double sided timber palisade fence 1.8 m high		detail number
			3·6
	scale 1:10	approved	date

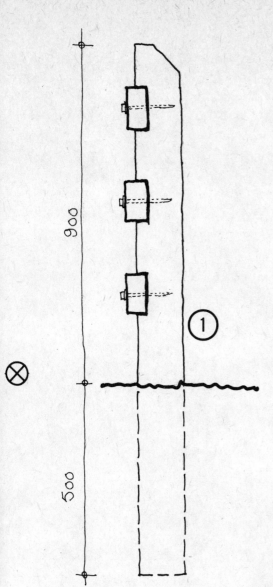

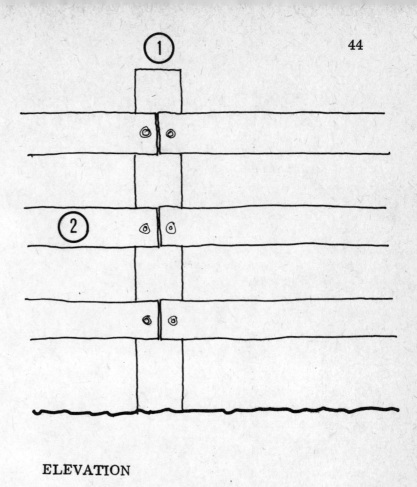

44

ELEVATION

1. 100 mm x 125 mm oak posts with weathered top with 25 mm rebates to receive rails as shown. Posts to be set in an augered hole at 1.8 m centres and backfilled with well rammed excavated material.

2. 100 mm x 50 mm oak rails fixed to posts as shown with 10 mm diameter galvanized drive screws 125 mm long. Rail ends drilled before fixing.

office stamp	project		cost index
			548
	drawing EXTERNAL WORKS DETAIL Timber post and rail fence		detail number
			3·7
	scale 1:10	approved	date

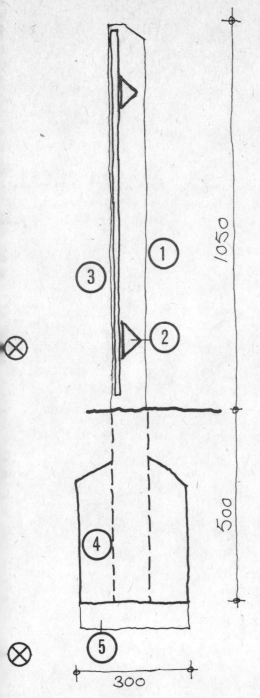

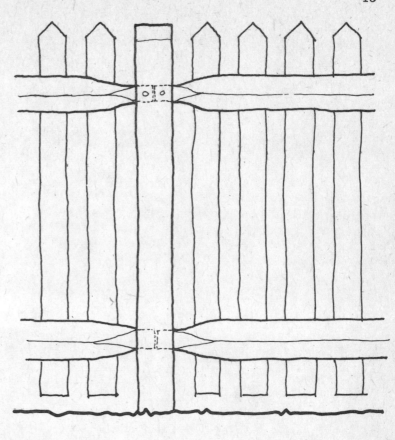

45

ELEVATION

1. 75 mm x 75 mm oak posts morticed to receive arris rails as required by BS 1722 Part 5. Posts at 1.8m centres.

2. 75 mm x 75 mm triangular arris rail ends shaped to fit mortices. Top rail only to have 15 mm diameter oak peg fixing.

3. 75 mm x 25 mm oak pailings fixed to rails at 125 mm centres with 2 no. 50 mm galvanized nails per rail.

4. 300 mm x 300 mm x 300 mm concrete surround. 1:6 mix

5. 50 mm coarse aggregate.

office stamp	project		cost index
			503
	drawing EXTERNAL WORKS DETAIL Timber palisade fence 1050 mm high		detail number
			3·8
	scale 1:10	approved	date

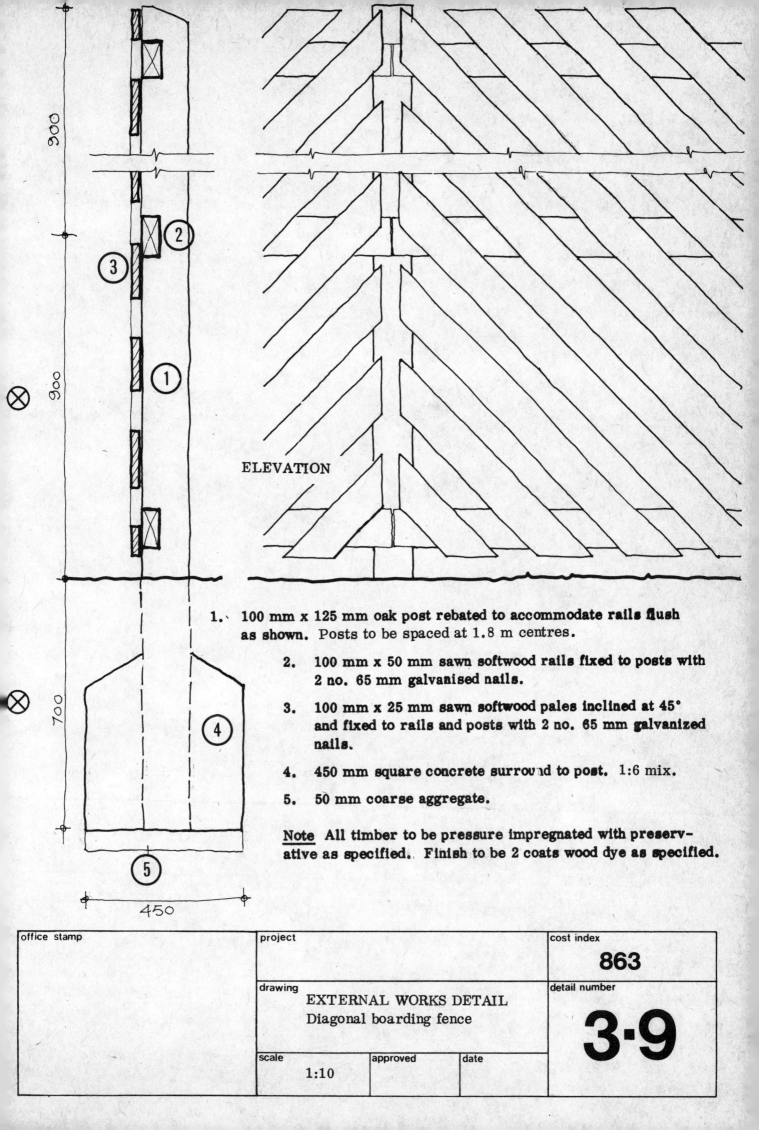

ELEVATION

900

900

700

450

1. 100 mm x 125 mm oak post rebated to accommodate rails flush as shown. Posts to be spaced at 1.8 m centres.

2. 100 mm x 50 mm sawn softwood rails fixed to posts with 2 no. 65 mm galvanised nails.

3. 100 mm x 25 mm sawn softwood pales inclined at 45° and fixed to rails and posts with 2 no. 65 mm galvanized nails.

4. 450 mm square concrete surround to post. 1:6 mix.

5. 50 mm coarse aggregate.

Note All timber to be pressure impregnated with preservative as specified. Finish to be 2 coats wood dye as specified.

office stamp	project		cost index
			863
	drawing		detail number
	EXTERNAL WORKS DETAIL Diagonal boarding fence		**3·9**
	scale	approved	date
	1:10		

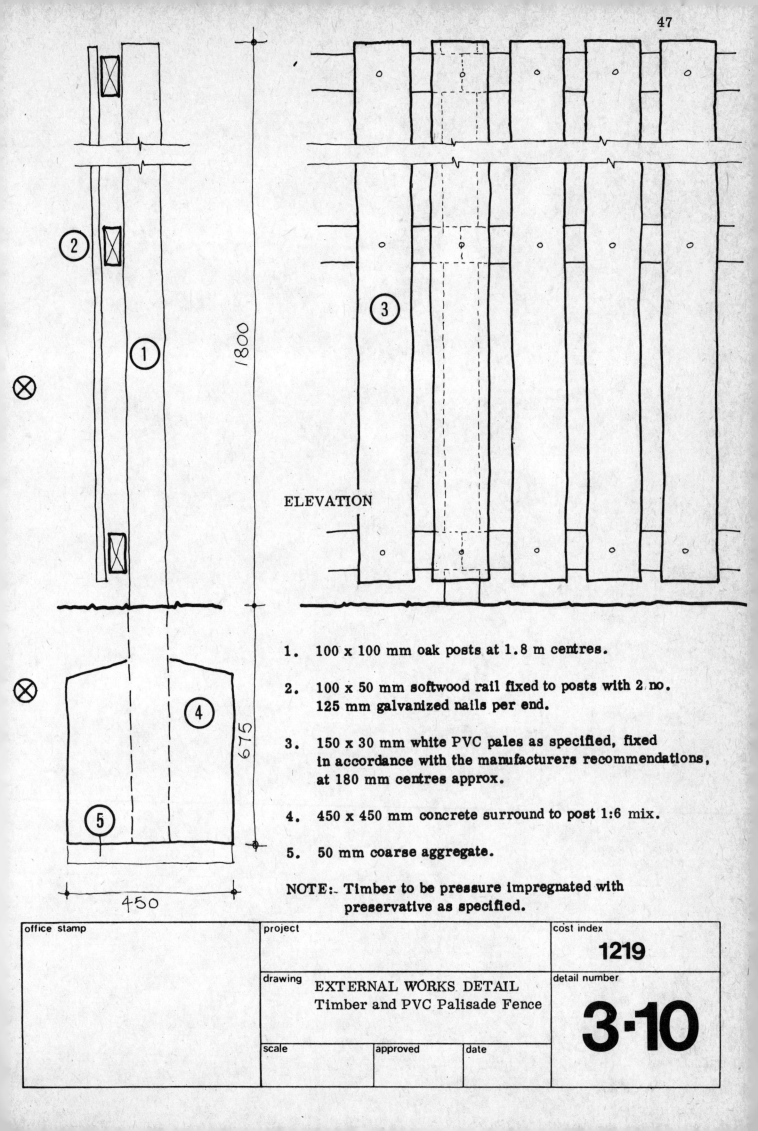

47

ELEVATION

1. 100 x 100 mm oak posts at 1.8 m centres.

2. 100 x 50 mm softwood rail fixed to posts with 2 no.
    125 mm galvanized nails per end.

3. 150 x 30 mm white PVC pales as specified, fixed
    in accordance with the manufacturers recommendations,
    at 180 mm centres approx.

4. 450 x 450 mm concrete surround to post 1:6 mix.

5. 50 mm coarse aggregate.

NOTE:- Timber to be pressure impregnated with
       preservative as specified.

office stamp	project		cost index
			1219
	drawing	EXTERNAL WORKS DETAIL Timber and PVC Palisade Fence	detail number
			3·10
	scale	approved	date

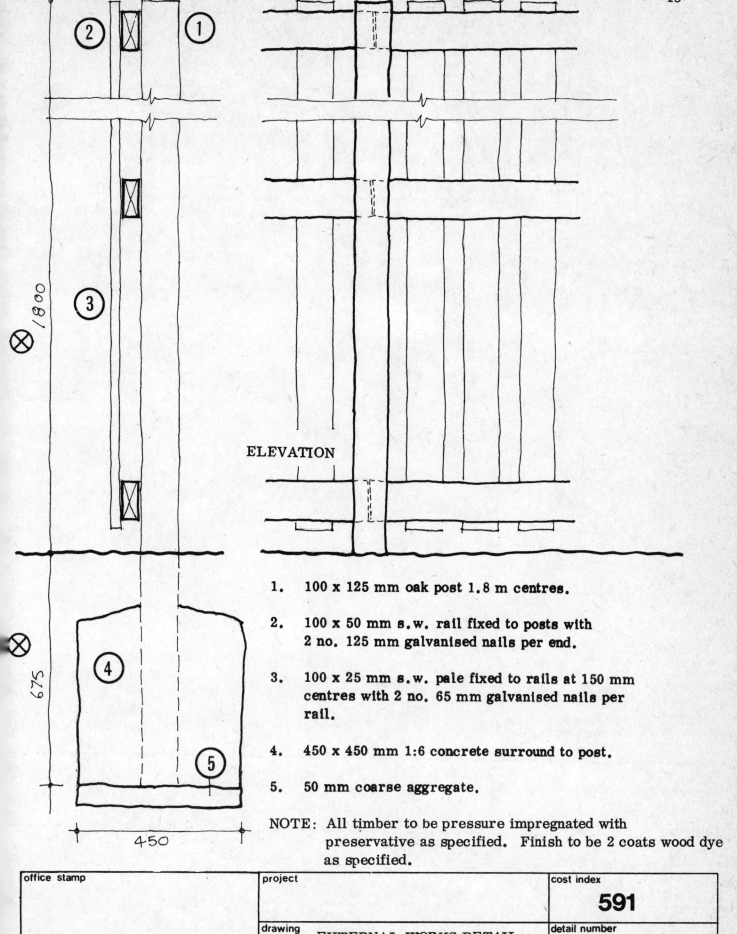

48

ELEVATION

1.   100 x 125 mm oak post 1.8 m centres.

2.   100 x 50 mm s.w. rail fixed to posts with 2 no. 125 mm galvanised nails per end.

3.   100 x 25 mm s.w. pale fixed to rails at 150 mm centres with 2 no. 65 mm galvanised nails per rail.

4.   450 x 450 mm 1:6 concrete surround to post.

5.   50 mm coarse aggregate.

NOTE: All timber to be pressure impregnated with preservative as specified. Finish to be 2 coats wood dye as specified.

office stamp	project		cost index
			591
	drawing	EXTERNAL WORKS DETAIL Timber palisade fence 1.8 m high	detail number
			3·11
	scale 1:10	approved	date

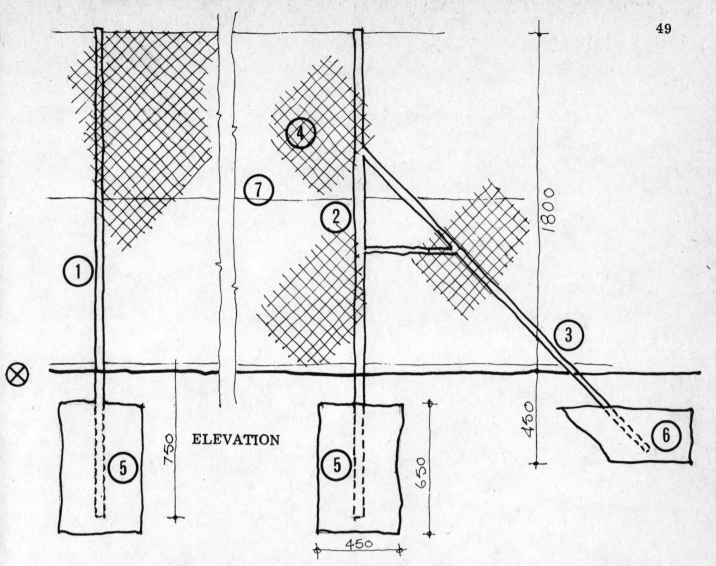

49

ELEVATION

1. 38 x 38 mm RHS 2.6 mm thick intermediate post, 3.0 m spacing, galvanised mild steel paint finish. Posts to be drilled to receive stirrup wire.

2. 50 x 50 mm RHS x 3.2 mm thick straining post at corners, ends and changes of direction and 150 m intervals on straight runs.

3. 25 mm x 25 mm RHH x 20 mm thick strut and brace.

4. Chain link fence wire to comply with BS 4102, plastic coated, 50 mm mesh. Heavy grade.

5. 450 x 450 x 650 mm concrete foundation to posts, concrete mix 1:6.

6. 450 x 300 x 300 concrete foundation to strut concrete mix 1:6.

7. Plastic coated line wire 3.0 mm diameter core.

Note Winding brackets, stretcher bars, and other fittings and materials shall be as specified in BS 1722 Part 1.

office stamp	project		cost index
			128
	drawing EXTERNAL WORKS DETAIL Chain link fence 1.8 m high		detail number
			3·12
	scale 1:20	approved	date

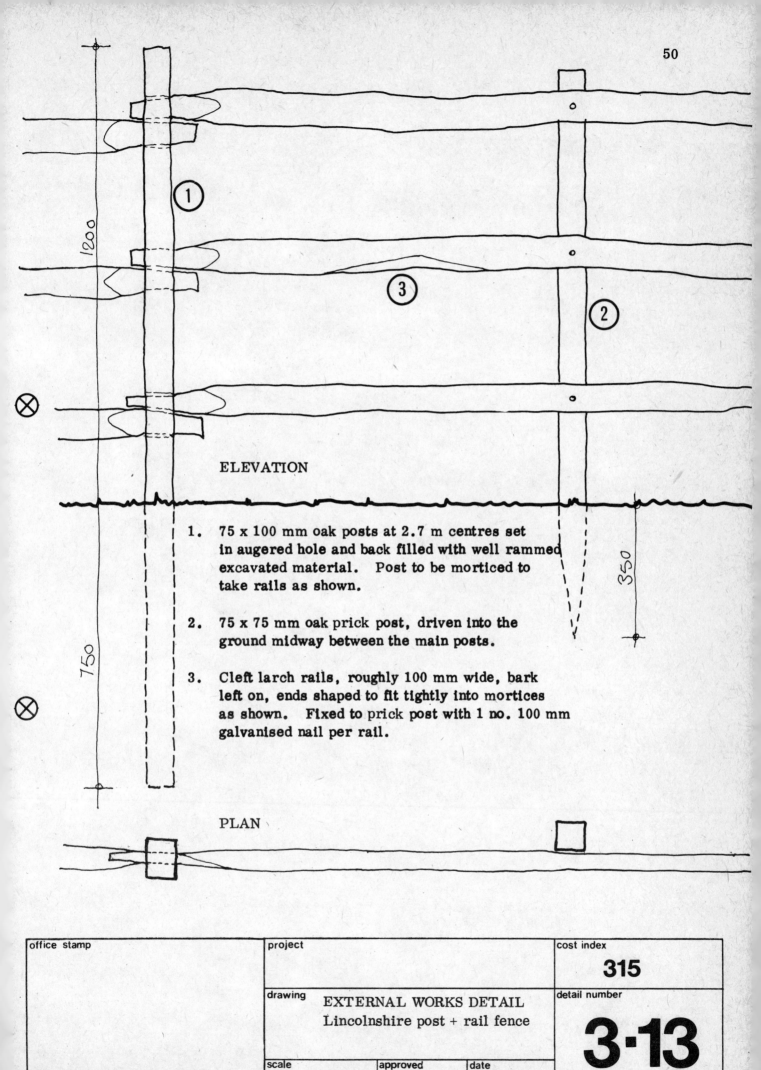

50

ELEVATION

1200

750

350

1. 75 x 100 mm oak posts at 2.7 m centres set in augered hole and back filled with well rammed excavated material.   Post to be morticed to take rails as shown.

2. 75 x 75 mm oak prick post, driven into the ground midway between the main posts.

3. Cleft larch rails, roughly 100 mm wide, bark left on, ends shaped to fit tightly into mortices as shown.   Fixed to prick post with 1 no. 100 mm galvanised nail per rail.

PLAN

office stamp	project		cost index
			315
	drawing	EXTERNAL WORKS DETAIL Lincolnshire post + rail fence	detail number
			3·13
	scale 1:10	approved	date

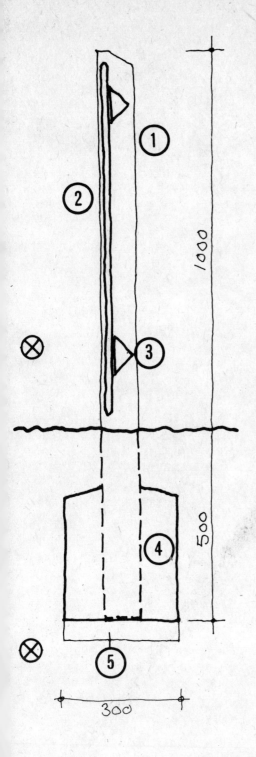

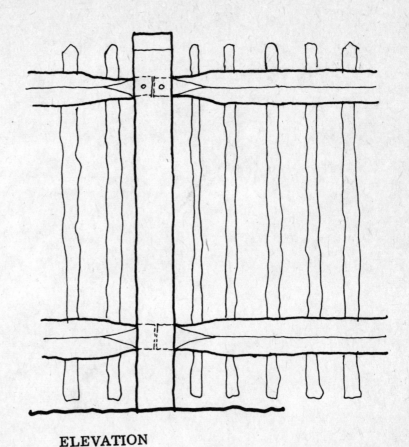

51

ELEVATION

1. 100 x 100 mm oak post at 2.7 m centres morticed as required by BS 1722, pt 5.

2. Cleft chestnut pales to BS 1722, pt 4, para. 2.2; distance between pales to be 75 mm. Fixing to be 65 mm galvanised nails.

3. 75 x 75 triangular arris, rail ends shaped as shown to fit mortice in posts. Top rails only secured by 15 mm diameter oak dowel.

4. 300 x 300 concrete surround to post, concrete mix 1:6.

5. 50 mm coarse aggregate.

NOTE: Timber posts shall be pressure impregnated with preservative as specified.

office stamp	project		cost index
			220
	drawing	EXTERNAL WORKS DETAIL Cleft chestnut fence 1.0 m high	detail number
			3·14
	scale 1:10	approved	date

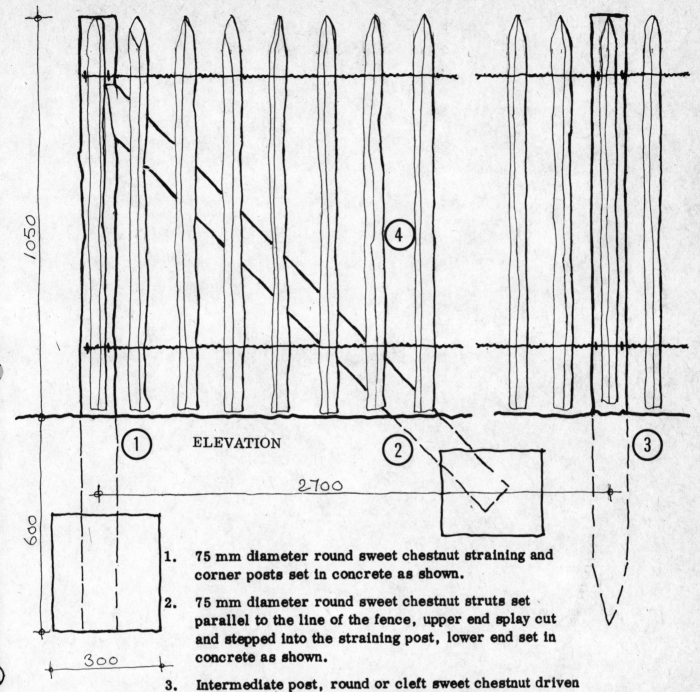

1050

600

300

2700

ELEVATION

1. **75 mm diameter round sweet chestnut straining and corner posts set in concrete as shown.**

2. **75 mm diameter round sweet chestnut struts set parallel to the line of the fence, upper end splay cut and stepped into the straining post, lower end set in concrete as shown.**

3. **Intermediate post, round or cleft sweet chestnut driven into ground at 2.7 m maximum centres.**

4. **Cleft chestnut pales wired together and stapled to posts.**

Note All timber and fittings are to conform to BS 1722 : Part 4.

office stamp	project	cost index
		100
	drawing	detail number
	EXTERNAL WORKS DETAIL	
	Cleft chestnut pale and wire	**3·15**
	fence 1050 mm high	
	scale	approved	date	
	1:10			

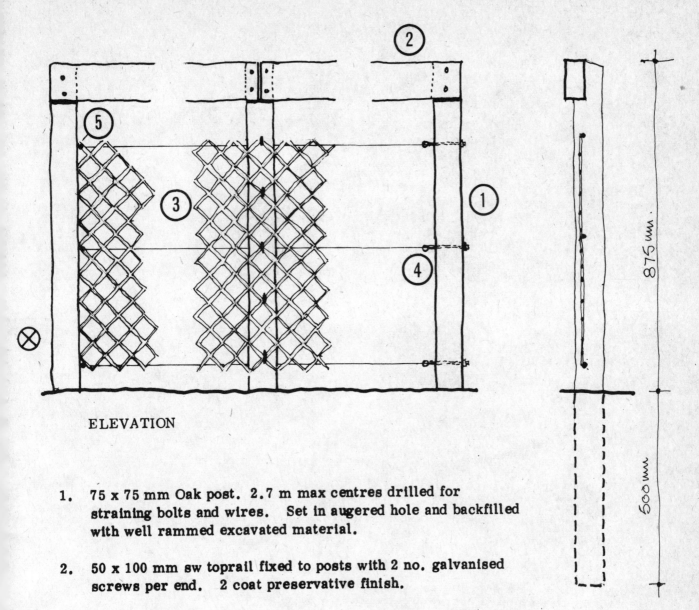

53

ELEVATION

1. 75 x 75 mm Oak post. 2.7 m max centres drilled for
    straining bolts and wires.   Set in augered hole and backfilled
    with well rammed excavated material.

2. 50 x 100 mm sw toprail fixed to posts with 2 no. galvanised
    screws per end.   2 coat preservative finish.

3. 610 mm "Netlon" plastic netting 50 mm diamond mesh,
    colour green.   Complete with plastic covered straining wires.
    Netting to be stapled to end and intermediate posts at 100 mm
    centres, and tied to straining wire with 2.0 mm diameter tie wires.

4. 125 mm galvanised eye bolts with washers and nuts.

5. 15 mm diameter galvanised eye screw.

office stamp	project		cost index
			148
	drawing	EXTERNAL WORKS DETAIL	detail number
		Timber and plastic mesh fence	
		875 mm high	**3·16**
	scale	approved	date
	1:10		

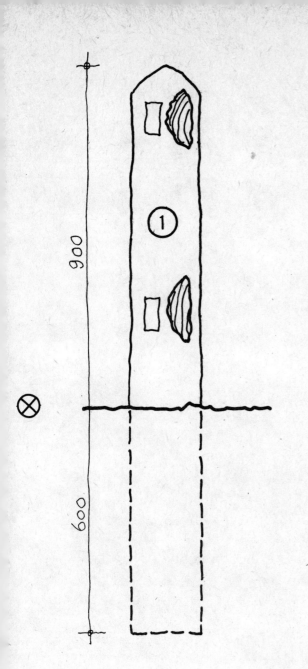

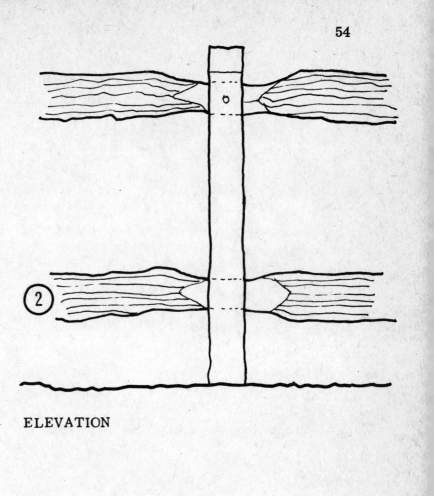

54

ELEVATION

PLAN

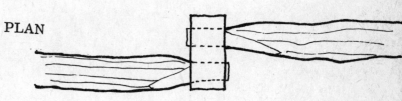

1. 200 mm x 75 mm sawn oak posts, with 50 mm x 75 mm double through mortices as shown, set in augered holes at 2.7 m maximum centres, and backfilled with well rammed excavated material.

2. Cleft oak rails, bark left on, roughly 125 mm on face, ends shaped to completely fill mortices in posts. Top rails secured by 15 mm diameter oak dowels.

office stamp	project	cost index
		253
	drawing EXTERNAL WORKS DETAIL Two rail Sussex fence 900 mm high	detail number
		3·17
	scale 1:10	approved	date	

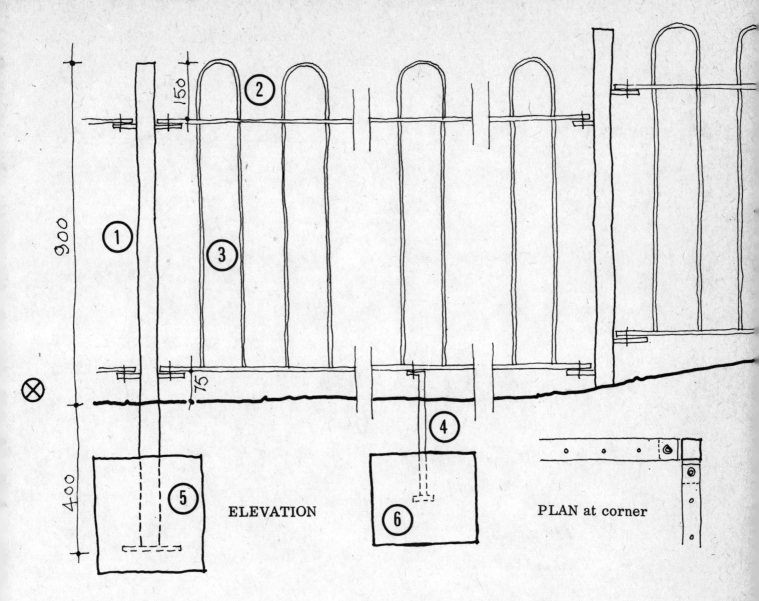

ELEVATION   PLAN at corner

1. 50 x 50 mm RHS standards 2.7 m spacing with welded lugs, capping plate, + 150 mm x 150 mm foot plate. All galvanised after manufacture and paint finished.

2. 50 x 10 mm galvanised mild steel flat, set screw fixed to standard lugs, paint finish.

3. 13 mm diameter mild steel bars with bow tops galvanised and paint finish.

4. 50 x 10 mm centre lug welded to bottom member at 900 mm centres.

5. 300 x 300 x 300 mm 1:6 concrete foundation.

6. 300 x 300 x 200 mm 1:6 concrete foundation.

office stamp	project		cost index **836**
	drawing **EXTERNAL WORKS DETAIL** Bow topped steel fence 900 mm high		detail number **3·18**
	scale **1:10**	approved date	

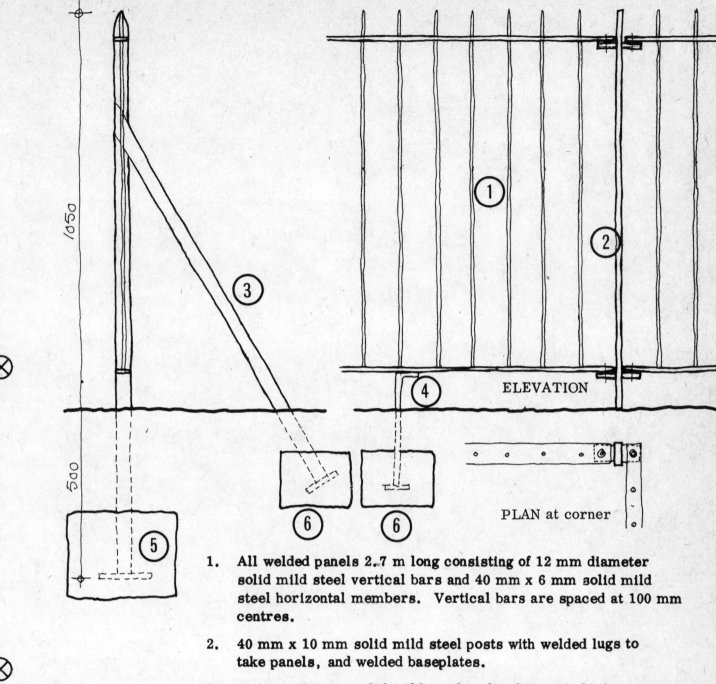

ELEVATION

PLAN at corner

1. All welded panels 2.7 m long consisting of 12 mm diameter solid mild steel vertical bars and 40 mm x 6 mm solid mild steel horizontal members. Vertical bars are spaced at 100 mm centres.

2. 40 mm x 10 mm solid mild steel posts with welded lugs to take panels, and welded baseplates.

3. 40 mm x 10 mm solid mild steel inclined stays bolted to posts.

4. 40 mm x 10 mm solid mild steel ground supports welded to bottom member. 2 no. per panel.

5. 300 mm x 300 mm x 300 mm concrete foundation. 1:6 mix.

6. 200 mm x 200 mm x 200 mm concrete foundation. 1:6 mix

Note All metal work to be galvanized after manufacture and paint finished.

office stamp	project		cost index
			667
	drawing EXTERNAL WORKS DETAIL Vertical bar steel fence 1050 mm high		detail number
			3·19
	scale 1:10	approved	date

58

4.0   LOW RAILS

a). Low Timber Rails

Timber Type and Size

Because of their height (up to 400 mm) low rails should be designed
bearing in mind their potential use for sitting and balancing on.   These
activities should either be discouraged or catered for by the design.

Post Spacing, Depth of Insertion

Because of the activities mentioned previously post centres are closer
than for real barrier fencing, usually 1.0 m to 1.5 m.

Post insertion depth of 300 mm is sufficient for pedestrian uses when
used with a concrete surround.   Where low timber rails are used for
controlling vehicular traffic an insertion depth of 750 mm will be
required.

Joints in Top Rail

The solution to the problem will vary with the design.   The following
general points should be observed.

1). Lapped or scarfed joints are preferable.

2). Bolts or screws should not be inserted within 25 mm of board ends.

3). Where the rail consists of two or more members, the joints in each
    should be staggered.

Corner Detail and Changes in Direction

Where corner and changes in direction are infrequent, the best solution
is to duplicate the post support.   Where a top rail is used adequate
bearing must be arranged for a mitred joint.

b). Low Metal Rails

Size of Rails

The remarks made in regard to timber low rails apply equally to
metal low rails.

Spacing of Standards

Metal low rail standards are generally spaced at 1.2 m centres.
A surround of concrete must be used because of the small surface
area of metal sections.

59

Metal Protection and Finish

The points made in Section 3 (metal fencing) apply.

Joints and Changes in Direction

Rails can be all shop welded construction made with a loose end
to the rail, which is jointed on site using a screwed sleeve or plate.

Changes in direction with metal rails are usually made in the rail;
the space between the standards should be closed to increase support
at this point.

REFERENCES

E and F. N. Spon Ltd.
   Spon's Landscape Handbook

NBA + 'Building' Commodity File
   Components (90) Section 02

4.0   LOW RAILS

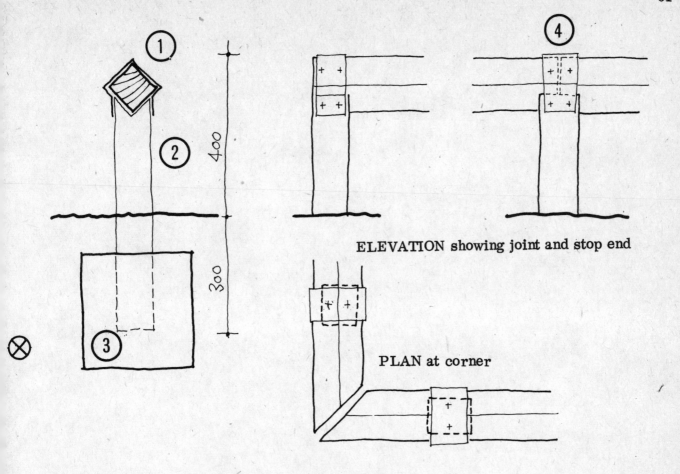

ELEVATION showing joint and stop end

PLAN at corner

1. 100 x 100 mm sawn oak top rail

2. 100 x 100 mm sawn oak posts, 1.5 m maximum spacing, ends shaped to receive top rail. Buried ends to be creosote impregnated as specified.

3. 300 x 300 x 300 mm concrete foundation to post, 1:6 mix.

4. 100 mm wide zinc strap. 37 mm galvanized clout nail fixing.

office stamp	project	cost index
		105
	drawing — EXTERNAL WORKS DETAIL Timber rail 400 mm high	detail number **4·1**
	scale — 1:10 — approved — date	

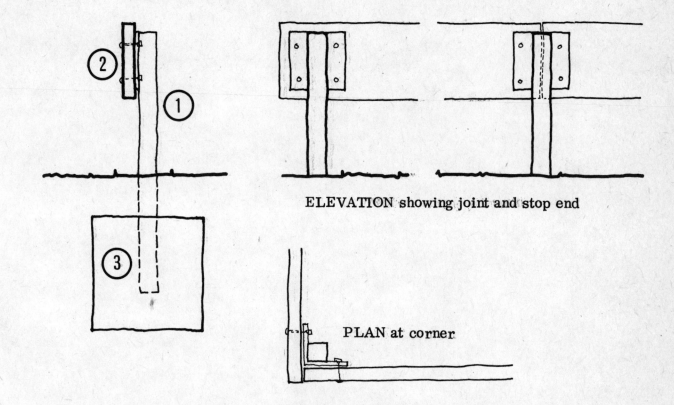

ELEVATION showing joint and stop end

PLAN at corner

1. 50 mm x 50 mm mild steel hollow section tube. Welded capping to top and with 150 mm x 150 mm x 6 mm mild steel plate welded to uprights and drilled to take bolts for rails. Corner posts to have fixing plate welded as shown. Paint finish.

2. 194 mm x 38 mm soft wood rail bolted to fixing plates with 10 mm x 50 mm sherardized coach bolts as shown. Soft wood to be pressure impregnated with preservative as specified. Finish to be 2 coat wood dye as specified

3. 300 mm x 300 mm x 300 mm 1:6 concrete surround to posts.

office stamp	project		cost index
			100
	drawing	EXTERNAL WORKS DETAIL Low timber and steel rail	detail number
			4·2
	scale 1:10	approved	date

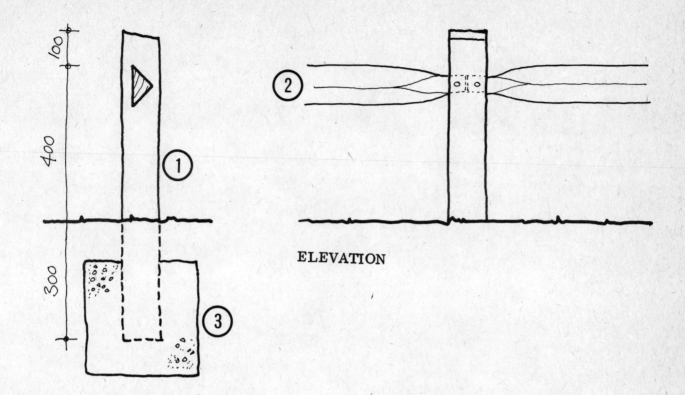

63

100

400

300

ELEVATION

1. 100 mm x 100 mm oak posts at 1.5 m centres morticed to take rails as required by BS 1722, pt. 5.

2. 75 mm x 75 mm oak triangular arris rails, ends roughly shaped to fit mortices. 15 mm diameter oak peg fixing.

3. 300 mm x 300 mm x 300 mm concrete surround to post, 1:6 concrete mix.

office stamp	project		cost index
			133
	drawing	EXTERNAL WORKS DETAIL	detail number
		Low timber rail	**4·3**
	scale 1:10	approved	date

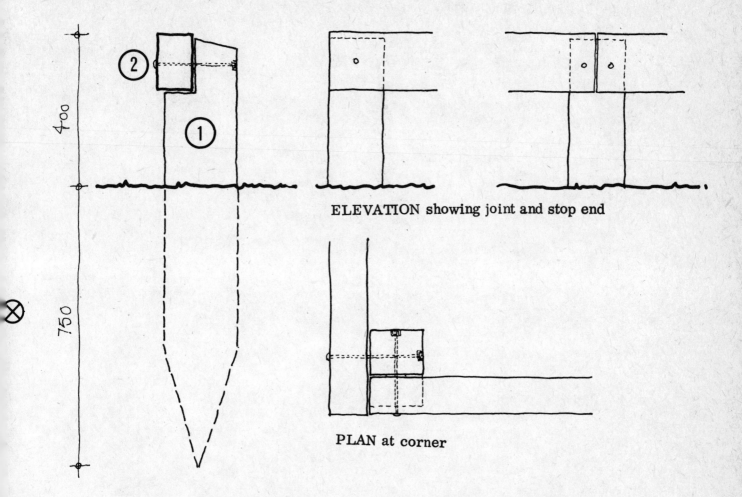

64

400

750

ELEVATION showing joint and stop end

PLAN at corner

1. 200 x 150 mm oak uprights at 1.0 m centres set in augered hole and back filled with well rammed excavated material. Top of upright shaped to take rail as shown.

2. 100 mm x 150 mm oak rail bolted to upright with 225 mm x 15 mm coach bolt. Nut to be recessed.

office stamp	project		cost index
			235
	drawing EXTERNAL WORKS DETAIL Low timber rail		detail number
			4.4
	scale 1:10	approved	date	

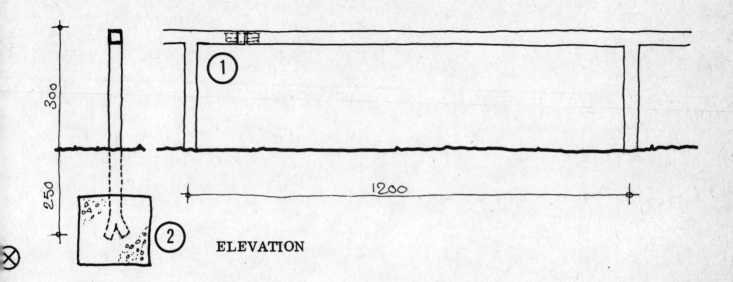

65

ELEVATION

1. 32 mm square section galvanized hollow steel tube; all welded construction with uprights at 1.2 m centres; sections connected by internal expanding spigot. Paint finish.

2. 300 mm x 300 mm x 300 mm concrete surround to uprights.

NOTE:

Steel tubing to be to
B.S. 4 part 2
Galvanizing to be to B.S. 729

office stamp	project		cost index
			126
	drawing	EXTERNAL WORKS DETAIL Low metal rail	detail number
			4.5
	scale 1:10	approved	date

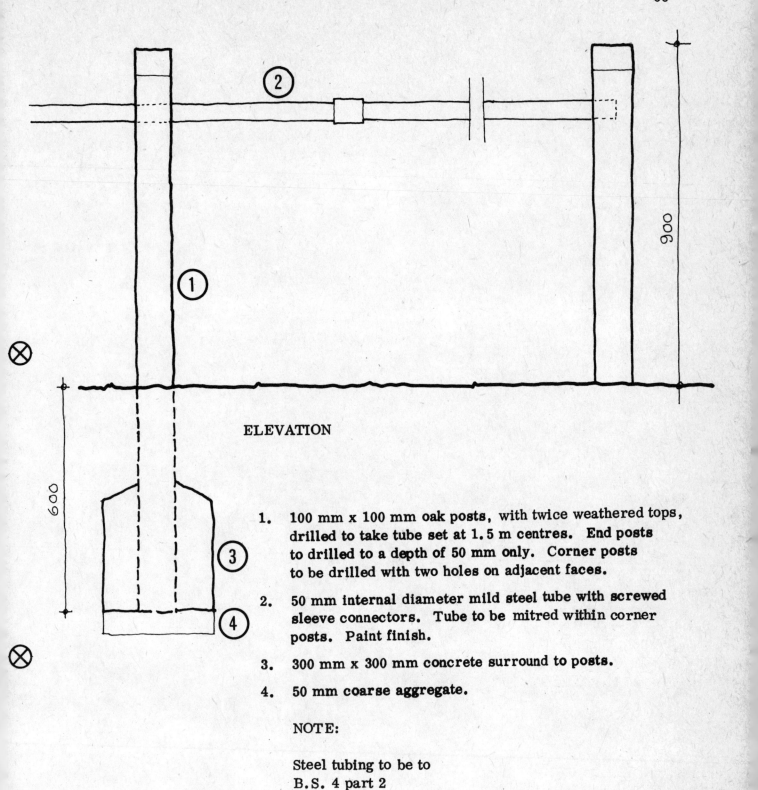

66

ELEVATION

1. 100 mm x 100 mm oak posts, with twice weathered tops,
drilled to take tube set at 1.5 m centres. End posts
to drilled to a depth of 50 mm only. Corner posts
to be drilled with two holes on adjacent faces.

2. 50 mm internal diameter mild steel tube with screwed
sleeve connectors. Tube to be mitred within corner
posts. Paint finish.

3. 300 mm x 300 mm concrete surround to posts.

4. 50 mm coarse aggregate.

NOTE:

Steel tubing to be to
B.S. 4 part 2

office stamp	project		cost index
			298
	drawing EXTERNAL WORKS DETAIL Timber and steel tube rail		detail number
			4·6
	scale 1:10	approved	date

5.0 PEDESTRIAN PAVING

Treatment of Sub-grade

The sub-grade should be well compacted either by hand or mechanical means. The required contour of the paving is obtained by shaping the sub-grade.

Base

The base is usually hardcore compacted with a 3 tonne roller or a 508 kg vibrating roller.

Wearing Course

Wearing courses can be divided into 4 categories.

i) Flexible (asphalt, bitumen or tar macadam, hoggin)

Flexible paving usually consists of two courses, a base course and a wearing course of a binder with varying sizes of aggregate. Aggregate size for wearing course should be 6 mm, base course aggregate size should be 20 mm. Usual thickness for base course is 50 mm and 6 - 20 mm for the wearing course.

ii) Small Rigid Units (bricks, stone sets, concrete units)

Small rigid units are usually laid on a base of consolidated hardcore or clinker with a 25 mm bed of sand or 15 mm sand/lime mortar. Joints are usually sand filled, or pointed with sand/lime mortar. Small concrete interlocking units are laid in contact on a dry sand bed.

iii) Large Rigid Unit (paving slabs)

Large rigid units can be laid over a consolidated base of clinker on a bed of sand or sand/lime mortar dabs.

iv) Rigid Pavement (insitu concrete)

Usually unreinforced concrete laid directly onto a consolidated sub-grade, or onto a base of consolidated hardcore, depending on ground conditions. Expansion joints must be incorporated at 6 m centres.

Joints

Tight, unfilled joints are only possible with units of regular size and shape such as pre-cast concrete paving flags or pre-cast concrete interlocking paving with which this method is usual.

69

Joints between paving brick, stone sets and natural pavings are best filled with a 1:3 cement mortar or a 1:4 lime mortar. The mortar is brushed dry into the joints and then watered. Use of this method reduces the risk of mortar staining the paving.

If plant or moss growth in the joints is to be encouraged, the joints can be filled with sifted topsoil or sand mixed with bone meal.

Edges

Flexible pavements must be contained by a rigid edge either a precast concrete edging with a concrete surround or a timber edging held by timber pegs.

Small rigid units should be contained by a row of units supported by a concrete backing.

Large rigid units need no edging where adjoining turfed or flexible paved areas. Where adjoining topsoil or planted areas an insitu concrete strip should be provided under the paving to prevent the base falling away.

Falls

The gradient of fall required to clear surface water varies according to the nature of the surface.

Recommended falls are

Concrete	1:60	Brick Paving	1:60
Bituminous Surfaces	1:40	Paving Slabs	1:70
Gravel	1:30	Public Pavements	1:50

REFERENCES

E and F. N. Spon Ltd.
  Spon's Landscape Handbook

Department of the Environment
  Design Bulletin 5
  Landscaping for Flats

British Standards Institute
  BS 368: 1971 Precast Concrete Flags
  BS 3690: 1970 Bitumens for Road Purposes

The Architectural Press, London
  C.C. Handisyde
  Hard Landscape in Brick 1976 Ch. 7
  J. Ashurst and F. G. Dimes
  Stone in Building 1977
  C. Tandy
  A. J. Handbook of Urban Landscape Information Sheet 34, 1972

NBA + 'Building' Commodity File
  Component File (90) section 01
  Paving: Precast Concrete

71

5.0 PEDESTRIAN PAVINGS

5.1   In-situ concrete paving
5.2   Asphalt paving
5.3   Sealed gravel paving
5.4   Compacted hoggin paving
5.5   Natural York stone paving
5.6   Pre-cast concrete flag paving
5.7   Pre-cast concrete exposed aggregate paving.
5.8   Brick paving - stretcher bond
5.9   Brick paving - herring bone
5.10 Cobbles loose laid
5.11 Granite sett paving
5.12 Granite sett paving
5.13 Brick paving - two panel type
5.14 Re-constructed stone sett paving
5.15 Cobbles laid flat

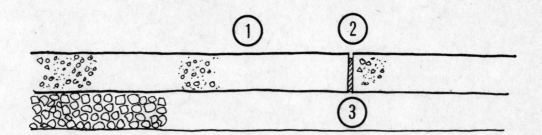

72

1. 100 mm concrete 1:2:4 mix tamped finish.

2. 10 mm expansion joints at 6 m intervals formed with
    impregnated sheet as specified, extending through the
    full depth of the slab.

3. 100 mm hardcore well consolidated with a 508 kg vibrating
    roller or equivalent.

office stamp	project		cost index
			147
	drawing EXTERNAL WORKS DETAIL In-situ concrete paving		detail number
			5·1
	scale 1:10	approved	date

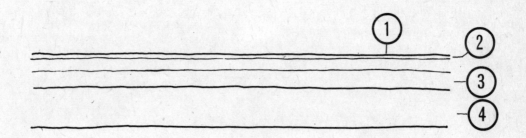

73

1. 10 mm pre-coated stone chippings rolled into surface.

2. 20 mm consolidated thickness hot rolled asphalt.

3. 40 mm consolidated thickness dense bitumen base course.
    (Department of Transport Specification cl. 903).

4. 100 mm hardcore well consolidated with a 508 kg vibrating
    roller or equivalent.

office stamp	project		cost index
			157
	drawing EXTERNAL WORKS DETAIL Asphalt paving		detail number
			5·2
	scale 1:10	approved	date

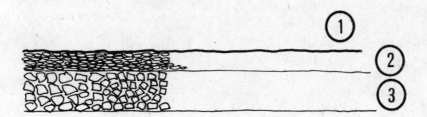

74

1. 6 mm rolled gravel topping with binder of cut-back bitumen to BS 3690.

2. 45 mm bitumen macadam, 20 mm aggregate.

3. 100 mm hardcore well consolidated with a 508 kg vibrating roller or equivalent.

office stamp	project		cost index
			167
	drawing	EXTERNAL WORKS DETAIL Sealed gravel paving	detail number
			5·3
	scale 1:10	approved	date

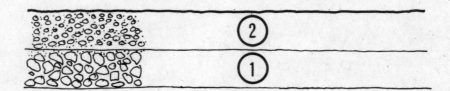

75

1. 100 mm compacted clean furnace clinker rolled with a 508 kg vibrating roller. Top surface blinded with fine hoggin, watered and rolled to a compacted thickness of 12 mm with a 508 kg vibrating roller.

2. Hoggin with maximum particle size of 50 mm, watered and rolled to a compacted thickness of 100 mm with a 508 kg vibrating roller.

office stamp	project		cost index
			100
	drawing	EXTERNAL WORKS DETAIL Compact hoggin paving	detail number
			5·4
	scale 1:10	approved	date

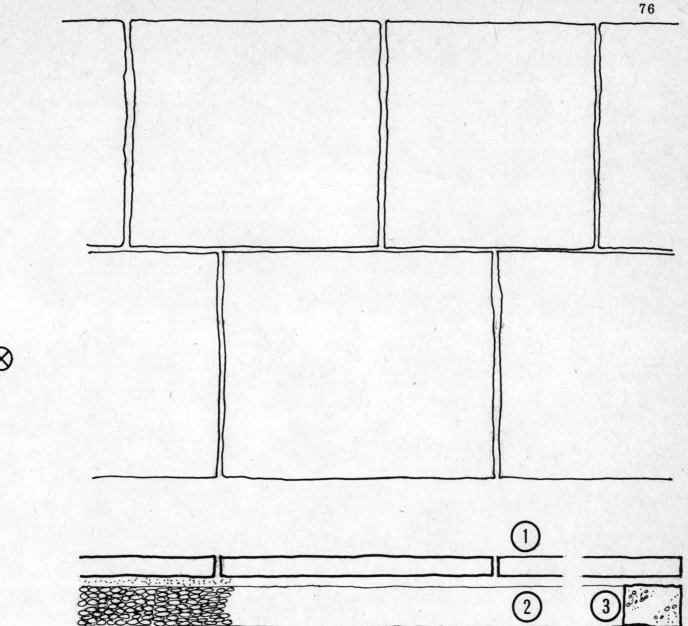

1. Natural York stone paving, sawn face and edges 600 mm wide, 38 mm thick in random lengths; laid breaking joint on 25 mm 1:4 lime mortar bed. Joints to be close butted.

2. 100 mm clinker consolidated with a 508 kg vibrating roller or equivalent.

3. 100 x 150 mm in-situ concrete edging to cultivated areas only.

office stamp	project		cost index
			1089
	drawing		detail number
	EXTERNAL WORKS DETAIL Natural York stone paving		
	scale	approved	date	**5·5**
	1:10			

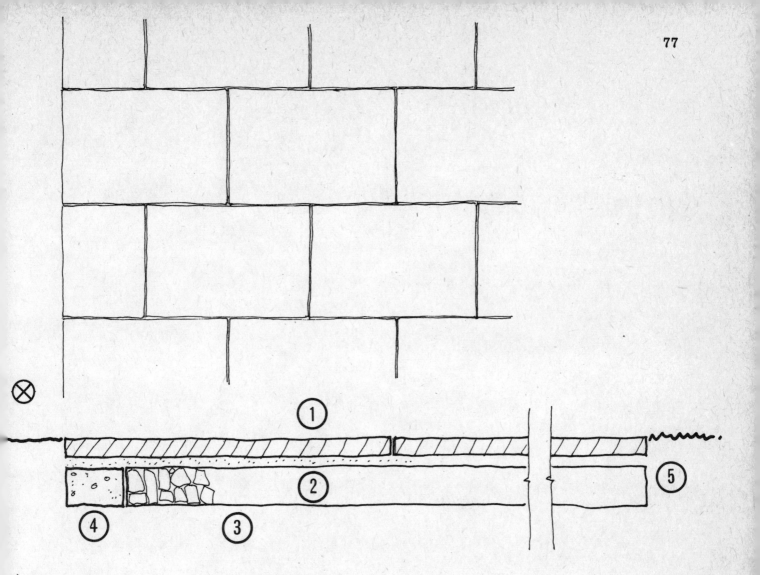

77

1. 50 mm x 600 x 900 mm precast concrete flags to
   BS 368: 1971, natural finish, butt joints.

2. 25 mm sand bed

3. 100 mm hardcore well consolidated with a 508 kg vibrating roller or equivalent.

4. 100 x 150 mm concrete edging to cultivated areas only

5. Detail of paving adjoining turfed area.

office stamp	project		cost index
			205
	drawing	EXTERNAL WORKS DETAIL Pre-cast concrete flag paving	detail number
			5·6
	scale 1:10	approved date	

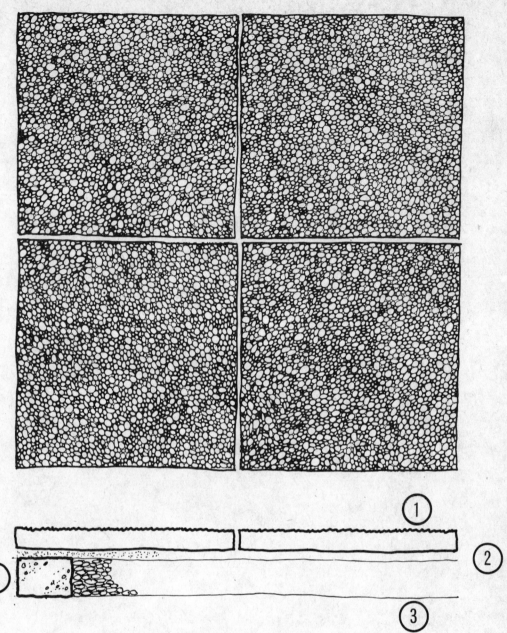

78

1. 600 mm x 600 mm precast concrete exposed aggregate paving slabs as specified laid close butted.

2. 25 mm 1:4 lime mortar bed.

3. 100 mm clinker base well consolidated with a 508 kg vibrating roller or equivalent.

4. 100 x 150 mm insitu concrete edging to cultivated areas only.

office stamp	project		cost index
			401
	drawing	EXTERNAL WORKS DETAIL Precast concrete exposed aggregate paving	detail number
			5·7
	scale	approved	date	
	1:10			

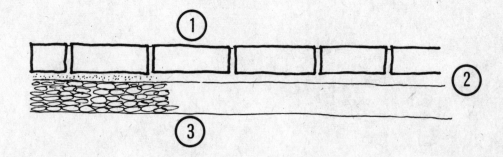

79

1. Paving bricks laid flat, joints filled with 1:4 lime mortar.

2. 25 mm 1:4 lime mortar bed.

3. 75 mm coarse clinker consolidated with 508 kg vibrating
    roller or equivalent.

office stamp	project		cost index **556**
	drawing EXTERNAL WORKS DETAIL Brick paving – stretcher bond		detail number **5·8**
	scale 1:10	approved	date	

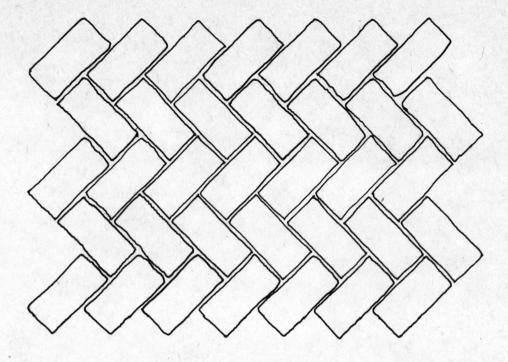

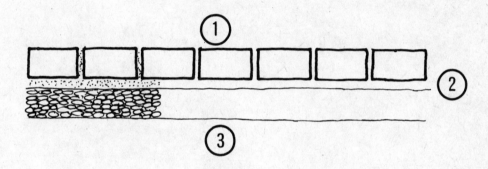

80

1. Bricks as specified, laid flat, in herringbone pattern as shown joints filled with 1:4 lime mortar brushed in dry and well watered.

2. 25 mm 1:4 lime mortar bed.

3. 75 mm coarse clinker consolidated with a 508 kg vibrating roller or equivalent.

office stamp	project		cost index
			602
	drawing	EXTERNAL WORKS DETAIL Brick paving - herringbone	detail number
			5·9
	scale 1:10	approved	date

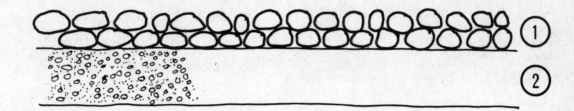

⊗

81

1. Kidney flint cobbles, size between 75 mm and 50 mm laid loose
    to a depth of 100 mm.

2. 150 mm hoggin, well consolidated by hand.

⊗

office stamp	project		cost index
			577
	drawing	EXTERNAL WORKS DETAIL Cobbles – loose laid	detail number
			5-10
	scale	approved	date
	1:10		

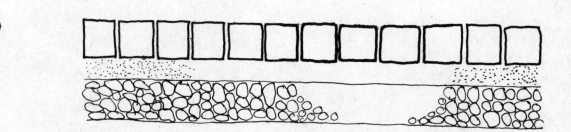

82

1. 102 x 102 x 102 mm second hand granite setts, joints fitted with 1:4 lime mortar brushed in dry and well watered.

2. 50 mm coarse sand bed.

3. 100 mm hardcore well consolidated with a 508 kg vibrating roller or equivalent.

office stamp	project		cost index
			862
	drawing	EXTERNAL WORKS DETAIL	detail number
		Granite sett paving	
	scale	approved	date	**5·11**
	1:10			

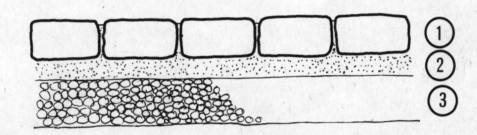

83

1. 102 mm x 102 mm x 204 mm second-hand granite setts, laid stretcher bond. Joints filled with 1:4 lime mortar brushed in dry and well watered.

2. 50 mm coarse sand bed.

3. 100 mm hardcore well consolidated with a 508 kg vibrating roller or equivalent.

office stamp	project		cost index
			908
	drawing EXTERNAL WORKS DETAIL Granite sett paving		detail number
			5·12
	scale 1:10	approved	date

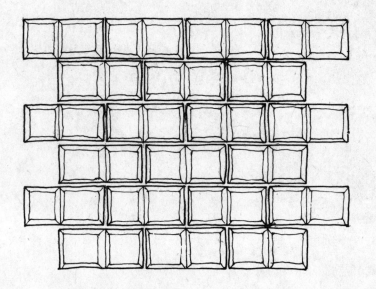

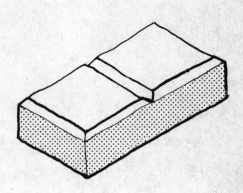

84

1. Staffordshire Blue engineering paving brick 50 mm thick with two raised panels as shown laid stretcher bond.   Joints to be fitted with 1:4 limemortar brushed in dry and well watered.

2. 25 mm 1:4 lime mortar bed.

3. 100 mm hardcore well consolidated with a 508 kg vibrating roller or equivalent.

office stamp	project	cost index
		785
	drawing **EXTERNAL WORKS DETAIL** Brick paving – two panel type	detail number **5-13**
	scale 1:10	approved	date	

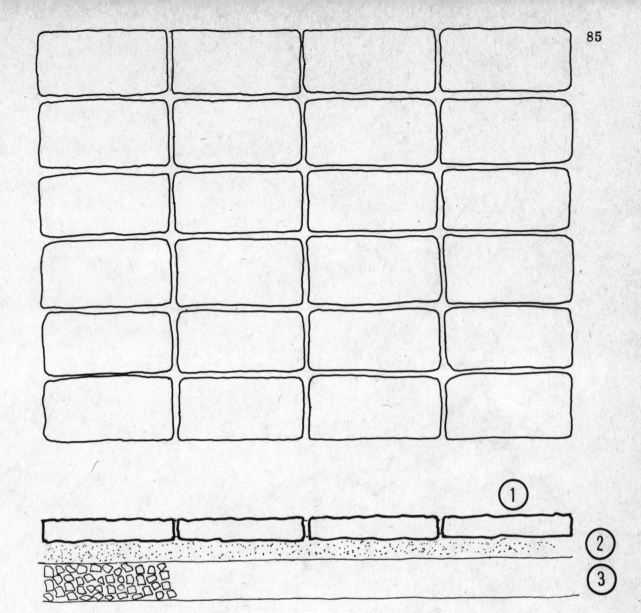

85

1. Reconstructed stone sett as specified 180 mm x 360 mm x 50 mm thick laid stack bond.   Joints to be filled with 1:4 lime mortar brushed in dry and well watered.

2. 50 mm coarse sand bed.

3. 100 mm hardcore well consolidated with a 508 kg vibrating roller or equivalent.

office stamp	project		cost index
			532
	drawing EXTERNAL WORKS DETAIL Reconstructed stone sett paving		detail number
			5·14
	scale 1:10	approved	date

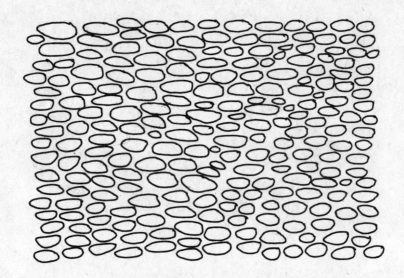

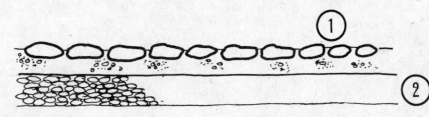

86

1. Kidney flint cobbles laid flat with their long axes parallel in 50 mm of 1:2:4 mix small aggregate concrete. Cobbles to be embedded by hand, tight butted, to a depth of half their thickness.

2. 75 mm coarse clinker base well consolidated with a 508 kg vibrating roller or equivalent.

office stamp	project		cost index
			791
	drawing	EXTERNAL WORKS DETAIL	detail number
		Cobbles laid flat	**5·15**
	scale 1:10	approved	date

88

6.0   VEHICULAR PAVING

The design of estate roads and their associated footpaths is subject to control by the Local Road Authority. For this reason any general design guidance will have to be modified in the light of local requirements.

Types of Road Construction

Road constructions can be divided into two categories -

i)   Flexible pavements

ii)   Rigid pavements

- both types of construction can be represented diagramatically as follows:-

$\longleftarrow$ wearing course

$\longleftarrow$ base course

$\longleftarrow$ road base

$\longleftarrow$ sub base

grade $\longrightarrow$

$\longleftarrow$ sub grade

In flexible pavement construction, the road base can be either lean-mix concrete, dense tarmacadam, dense bitumen macadam, dry bound macadam or wet mix macadam, soil-cement or a number of other materials. Each type of road base is specified in detail in the D.O.E. publication 'Specification for Road and Bridge Works'.

In rigid construction the road base is either reinforced or unreinforced concrete.

The sub-base material and thickness is dependent entirely on the stability of the subgrade and can be omitted altogether on very stable subgrades.

In rigid pavement construction the top surface of the concrete road base is the top surface of the finished road.

In flexible pavement construction a wearing course and a base course of either tarmacadam or bitumen macadam is then added to the road base. On lightly trafficked roads a single course , not less than 65 mm thick is sometimes used.

89

The method by which the thickness of each structural layer is determined is set out in Road Note 29.

A combination construction of continuously reinforced concrete with a bituminous surface is sometimes used for city streets, but is unlikely to be used on estate roads.

REFERENCES

Department of the Environment
  Road Note 29
  Specification for Road and Bridge Works
  Design Bulletin 5 'Landscaping for Flats'

The Architectural Press, London
  M. Gage and M. Vandenberg
  Hard Landscape in Concrete   Information Sheet 2, 1975

Countryside Commission
  Surfaces of Rural Car Parks

Asphalt and Coated Macadam Association
  Modern Flexible Road Construction
  The Types and Scope of Coated Macadam

NBA + 'Building' Commodity File
  Component File (90) Section 03

E and F. N. Spon
  Spon's Landscape Handbook

Department of Transport
  Specification for Road and Bridge Works
  Notes for guidance on the Specification for
  Road and Bridge Works

Cement and Concrete Association
  J. Knapton
  The Design of Concrete Block Roads   May 1976

90

6.0   VEHICULAR PAVINGS

6.1   Tarmacadam Road
6.2   Concrete Road
6.3   Exposed aggregate concrete paving
6.4   Sealed gravel paving
6.5   Mono slab grass/concrete paving
6.6   Mono Lok interlocking concrete paving
6.7   Grano sett paving

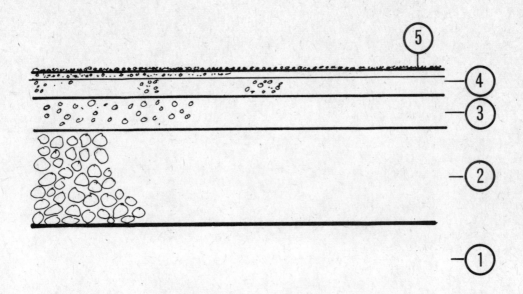

1. Subgrade compacted and shaped to the requirements of Department of Transport Specification (Clauses 608, 609).

2. Subbase 170mm granular material as DOT specification (clause 804) laid and compacted in accordance with clause 802.

3. Roadbase 80mm rolled asphalt to BS 594 laid and compacted to DOT specification (Clauses 704, 705).

4. Base course 50mm tar macadam to BS 802

5. Wearing course 20mm tar macadam to BS 802 surface dressed with 10mm gravel with binder of cut back bitumen to BS 3690.

office stamp	project		cost index
			239
	drawing	EXTERNAL WORKS DETAIL	detail number
		Tarmacadam road	**6·1**
	scale	approved	date
	1:10		

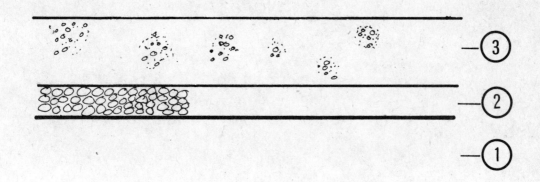

92

1. Subgrade shaped and compacted to Department of Transport Specification (Clauses 608, 609)

2. 80mm subbase Type 1 granular material as DOT specification (clause 803) laid and compacted in accordance with clause 802.

3. 170mm unreinforced concrete slab to DOT specification (clause 1004). Contraction joints to be provided at 6m intervals as DOT specification (clause 1009).

office stamp	project		cost index
			175
	drawing EXTERNAL WORKS DETAIL Concrete road		detail number
			6·2
	scale 1:10	approved	date	

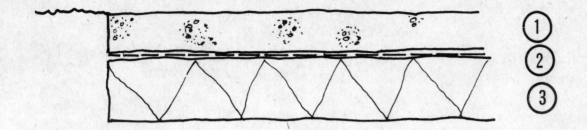

93

1.   100mm 1:2:4 concrete with 20mm maximum aggregate.
        Aggregate to be exposed by brushing and washing as specified.
        10mm construction joints to be incorporated every 6m.

2.   Building paper, lapped 100mm at joints on 25mm ash blinding.

3.   150mm hardcore well consolidated with 3 tonne roller or
        equivalent.

office stamp	project		cost index
			155
	drawing		detail number
	EXTERNAL WORKS DETAIL Exposed aggregate concrete paving		**6·3**
	scale	approved	date
	1:10		

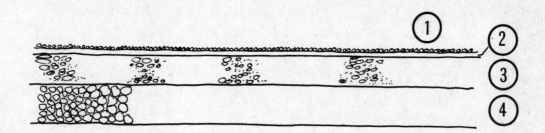

94

1. 15 mm of 10-6 mm Breedon gravel spread on a sprayed layer of cold bituminous emulsion and rolled with a 3 tonne roller

2. 15 mm of 12-10 mm Breedon gravel spread on a sprayed layer of cold bituminous emulsion and rolled with a 3 tonne roller.

3. 75 mm consolidated hoggin, rolled with 3 tonne roller.

4. 100 mm hardcore well consolidated with a 3 tonne roller or equivalent.

office stamp	project		cost index
			100
	drawing	EXTERNAL WORKS DETAIL Sealed gravel paving	detail number
	scale	approved date	**6·4**
	1:10		

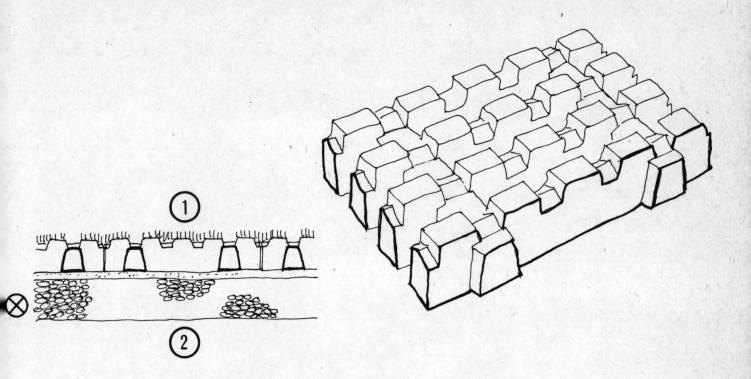

95

1. Monoslabs Type G, manufactured by Mono Concrete Limited
    and laid on 20 mm sand in accordance with their recommendations.
    Interstices to be filled with topsoil to a level of 25 mm below
    the upper surface of the slab and seeded with grass seed to
    BS 4428:1969 as specified.

2. 125 mm sub base granular material MOT Type 2
    (Specification 1969 cl. 804).

office stamp	project		cost index
			273
	drawing	EXTERNAL WORKS DETAIL Monoslab grass/concrete paving	detail number
			6·5
	scale	approved	date
	1:10		

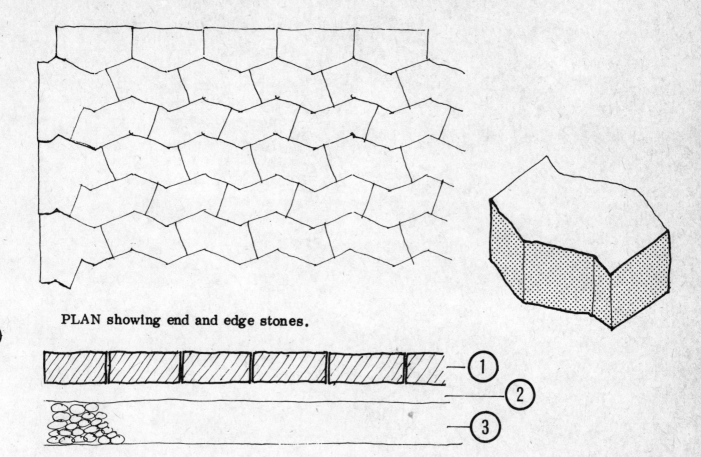

96

PLAN showing end and edge stones.

1. 80 mm Monolok concrete units, colour grey, manufactured by Mono Concrete Ltd. and laid in accordance with their recommendations. Units to be laid to falls of 1:60 plus curves shall be achieved by the use of 'curve sets' designed for the purpose.

2. 50 mm coarse sand bed.

3. 125 mm sub base granular material DOT spec. cl. 804

office stamp	project		cost index **206**
	drawing	EXTERNAL WORKS DETAIL Monolok interlocking paving	detail number **6-6**
	scale 1:10	approved	date

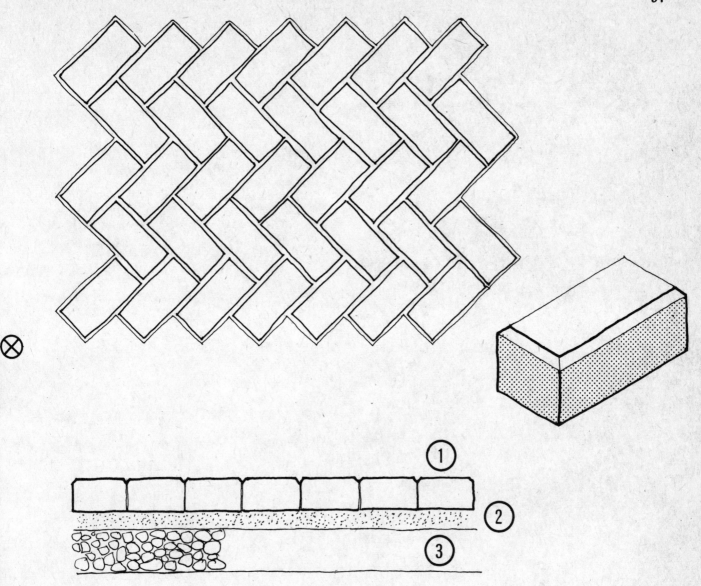

97

1. 80 mm thick 'Granosett' pre-cast paving block, natural colour manufactured by Redland Precast Ltd. and laid in accordance with their recommendations.

2. 50 mm coarse sand bed.

3. 125 mm sub-base granular material.   DOT spec. cl. 804

office stamp	project		cost index 163
	drawing EXTERNAL WORKS DETAIL Granosett paving		detail number 6·7
	scale 1:10	approved	date

7.0   STEPS AND RAMPS

Steps

External steps should have a rise of between 80 and 150 mm. The going should not be less than 300 mm; the maximum number of rises per flight should be 19. Landings should be between 1 and 2 m wide. If extensive use by old people is anticipated a hand rail should be provided.

Thought should be given to the retaining of the ground adjoining the steps, and to the incorporation of a mowing margin if necessary.

Ramps

Ramps should have a maximum gradient of 1:10. For wheelchairs the maximum should be 1:12. The surface should be non-slip and surface water should be shed across the ramp preferably into a drainage channel.

Ramp lengths should not exceed 10 m. Level landings should be provided at intervals.

Stepped Ramps

Stepped ramps can be used to reduce the apparent steepness of a long ramp. To allow easy negotiations by prams and wheelchairs, riser dimension should not exceed 100 mm and the tread dimension should not be less than 900 mm and preferably 1.5 m. Nosings of treads should be clearly defined by a change of colour or texture.

REFERENCES

E and F. N. Spon
 Spon's Landscape Handbook

The Architectural Press, London
 C. Tandy
 A. J. Handbook of Urban Landscape Information Sheet 35, 1972.

7.0 STEPS AND RAMPS

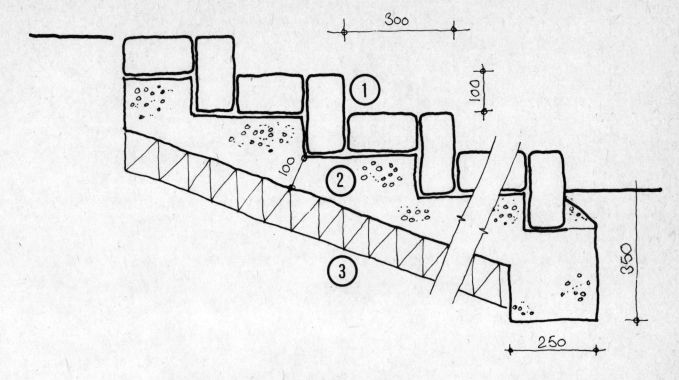

101

1. 200 x 100 second-hand granite setts bedded on 1:3 cement mortar, all joints pointed up.

2. In-situ concrete 1:8 mix.

3. 100 mm clean hardcore.

office stamp	project		cost index
			399
	drawing	EXTERNAL WORKS DETAIL Granite sett steps	detail number
			7·1
	scale	approved	date
	1:10		

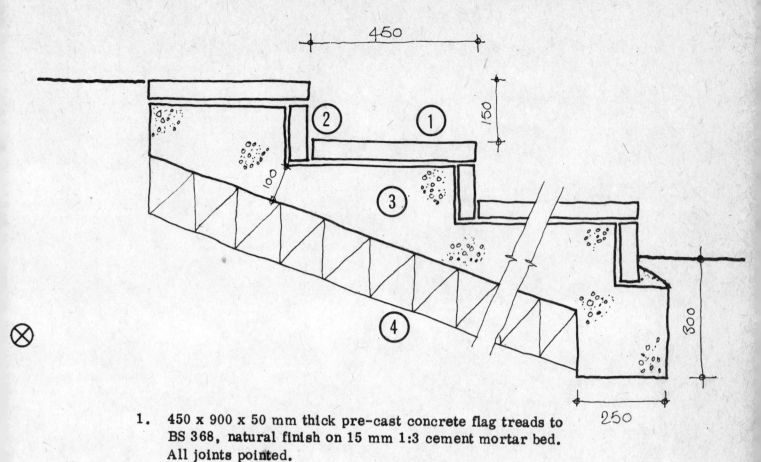

102

1.   450 x 900 x 50 mm thick pre-cast concrete flag treads to
     BS 368, natural finish on 15 mm 1:3 cement mortar bed.
     All joints pointed.

2.   200 x 900 x 50 mm thick pre-cast concrete edging to BS 340 figure 11
     natural finish on 15 mm 1:3 cement mortar bed.   All joints pointed.

3.   In-situ concrete 1:8 mix.

4.   100 mm clean hardcore.

office stamp	project		cost index
			180
	drawing	EXTERNAL WORKS DETAIL Pre-cast concrete flag steps	detail number
			7·2
	scale 1:10	approved	date

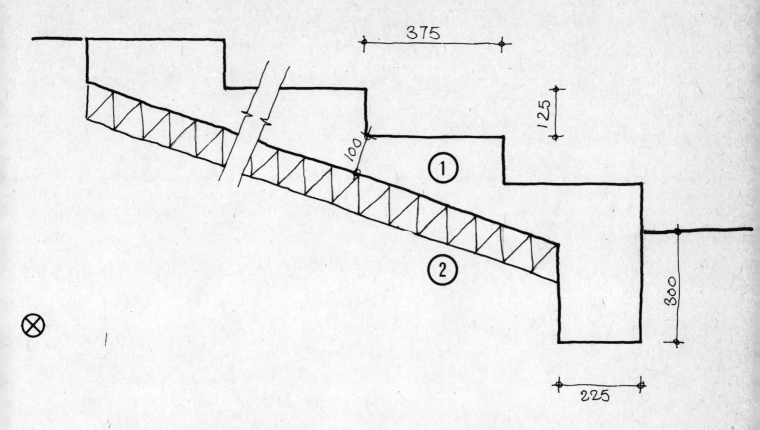

103

375

125

100

300

225

1. In-situ concrete steps. 1:2:4 mix, trowel finish.

2. 100 mm clean hardcore.

office stamp	project		cost index
			100
	drawing	EXTERNAL WORKS DETAIL In-situ concrete steps	detail number
			7·3
	scale 1:10	approved	date

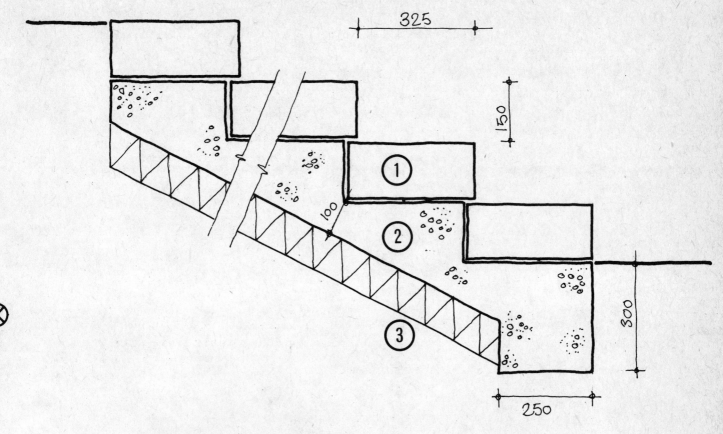

1. Reconstructed stone treads 350 x 150 mm on 1:3 cement mortar
    bed.   All joints pointed up.

2. In-situ concrete 1:8 mix.

3. 100 mm clean hardcore.

office stamp	project		cost index
			345
	drawing	EXTERNAL WORKS DETAIL	detail number
		Reconstructed stone steps	**7.4**
	scale	approved date	
	1:10		

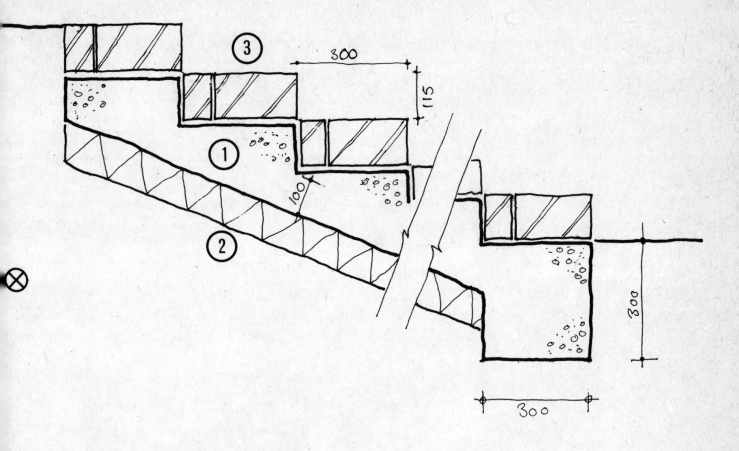

105

1.   Insitu concrete 1:8 mix.

2.   100mm clean hardcore.

3.   Bricks on edge as specified bedded in 1:3 cement mortar, all
        joints to be flush pointed.

office stamp	project		cost index
			255
	drawing	EXTERNAL WORKS DETAIL Brick paving steps	detail number
			7·5
	scale 1:10	approved	date

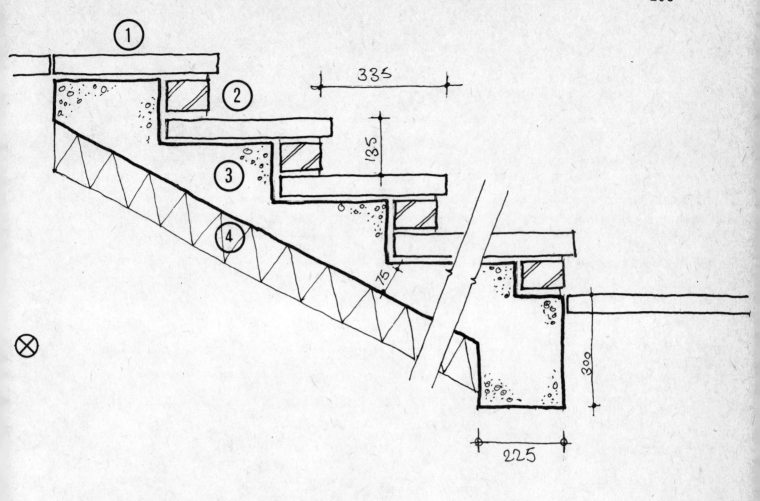

106

1. 50mm x 450mm precast concrete flags to BS 368 natural finish on 1:4 lime/sand bed.

2. Brick riser as specified in 1:4 lime/sand bed.

3. Insitu concrete 1:8 mix.

4. 100mm clean hardcore.

office stamp	project		cost index
			218
	drawing	EXTERNAL WORKS DETAIL Concrete flag and brick steps	detail number **7.6**
	scale 1:10	approved	date

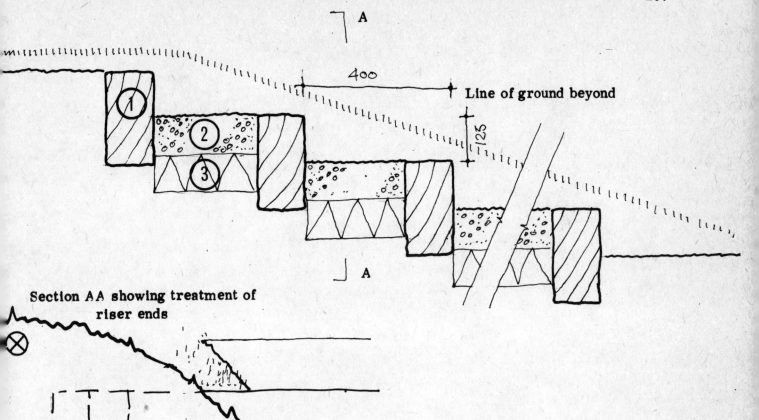

107

A

400

Line of ground beyond

125

A

Section AA showing treatment of riser ends

1. 125 x 250 mm railway sleeper riser bedded on consolidated subsoil.   Ends of sleeper buried as shown.

2. 100 mm coarse hoggin consolidated by hand.

3. 100 mm consolidated hardcore.

4. 100 x 100 x 400 mm preservative impregnated s.w peg nailed to sleeper

office stamp	project		cost index
			239
	drawing	EXTERNAL WORKS DETAIL Timber and hoggin steps	detail number
			7·7
	scale	approved	date
	1:10		

8.0   MOWING MARGINS, TRIMS, KERBS AND DRAINAGE CHANNELS

Mowing Margins

One of the critical aspects of using grass is the treatment of the edges
of areas of grass in order to avoid edge trimming.

Grass edges should be kept at least 225 mm away from all walls and other
obstructions, and should abut a hard edge.

The infill materials can be any material which will not support plant growth.

Loose gravel and hoggin should be used with discretion as their use implies
a high standard of maintenance.

Where possible the use of mowing strips can be avoided by planting against
walls.

Trims and Kerbs

Trims are necessary to retain the sub-strata of areas of paving and to
prevent the edges breaking away. Trims should be retained by a concrete
foundation and haunching.

Trims are also used to mark limits of ownership or to subdivide areas of
concrete paving.

Kerbs are necessary to control surface water drainage from roads and to
discourage the encroachment of vehicles onto the footpath. The usual
method of achieving this is to use a 125 x 250 mm precast concrete kerb.
There is no reason why other materials or other design approaches should
not be used. Any road kerb detail will have to be agreed with the adopting
authority.

A range of precast concrete kerbs and edgings is illustrated in BS 340: 1963.
Granite or flint aggregate may be specified.

Drainage Channels

Drainage channels are used when draining large areas of paving and when
draining ramps or paths contained between walls. The width of the channel
must be related to the size of the gully grating.

An alternative to surface channels is the use of a 'safticurb' section or
a glazed half round channel with a cast iron grating. Both types need a
high degree of maintenance to prevent silting up.

Falls should be between 1:200 for precast concrete materials and 1:60 for
brick and granite sett channels.

110

REFERENCES

E and F. N. Spon
  Spon's Landscape Handbook

Department of the Environment
  Housing Development Notes
  No. 4 Grass and Small Plants
  No. 11 Landscape of New Housing

British Standards Institute
  BS 340 : 1963 Pre-cast concrete kerbs, channels,
  edgings and quadrants
  BS 435 : 1931 Granite and Whinstone kerbs,
  channels and quadrants

The Architectural Press, London
  C. Tandy
  A. J. Handbook of Urban Landscape   Information Sheet 34, 1972
  C. C. Handisyde
  Hard Landscape in Brick Chapter 7, 1976

NBA + 'Building' Commodity File
  Components File (90) Section 02

111

8.0   MOWING MARGINS   TRIMS, KERBS AND DRAINAGE CHANNELS

8.1   Brick mowing margin
8.2   In-situ concrete mowing margin
8.3   Paving slab mowing margin
8.4   Hoggin mowing margin
8.5   Pre-cast concrete and channel
8.6   Pre-cast concrete flush kerb
8.7   Pre-cast concrete kerb
8.8   Granite sett kerb
8.9   Granite sett trim
8.10   Granite kerb
8.11   Brick kerb
8.12   Concrete and granite sett kerb
8.13   Pre-cast concrete edging
8.14   Granite sett trim
8.15   Brick edging
8.16   Brick work trim
8.17   Timber edging
8.18   Brick on edge edging
8.19   Safticurb drainage channel
8.20   Granite sett drainage channel
8.21   Dished concrete drainage channel
8.22   Brick drainage channel

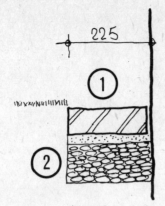

112

1. Paving brick laid flat on 25 mm coarse sand, joint mortar pointed.

2. 75 mm consolidated hardcore treated with an approved weed killer.

office stamp ⊗	project		cost index 512
	drawing EXTERNAL WORKS DETAIL Brick mowing margin.		detail number 8·1
	scale 1:10	approved	date	

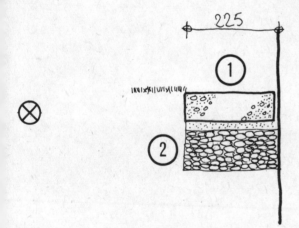

1. 75 mm insitu concrete on 25 mm sand bed. 10 mm expansion joints at 6 m intervals

2. 100 mm consolidated hardcore treated with an approved weed killer.

office stamp ⊗	project		cost index 379
	drawing EXTERNAL WORKS DETAIL In-situ concrete mowing margin		detail number 8·2
	scale 1:10	approved	date	

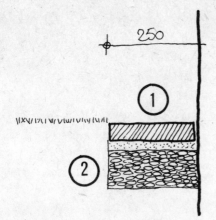

113

1. 50 x 250 mm precast concrete
    edging laid flat on 25 mm sand.
    Joints between slabs to be 1:3
    cement mortar pointed.

2. 100 mm consolidated hardcore treated
    with an approved weed killer.

office stamp	project		cost index
⊗			**456**
	drawing	EXTERNAL WORKS DETAIL Paving slab mowing margin	detail number
			8·3
	scale 1:10	approved	date

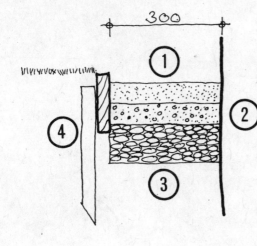

1. 50 mm fine gravel.

2. 50 mm consolidated coarse hoggin.;

3. 100 mm consolidated hardcore treated
    with an approved weed killer.

4. 150 x 38 mm treated S. W. board
    nailed to 38 x 38 mm x 400 mm
    pegs at 1200 mm centres.

office stamp	project		cost index
⊗			**479**
	drawing	EXTERNAL WORKS DETAIL Hoggin mowing margin	detail number
			8·4
	scale 1:10	approved	date

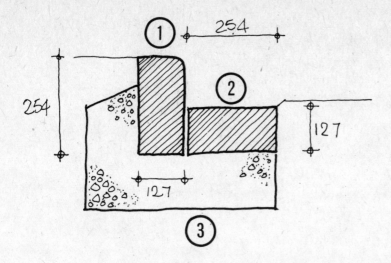

114

1. Precast concrete kerb to BS 340, Figure 2.

2. Precast concrete channel to BS 340, Figure 8.

3. 150 mm concrete base and backing, 1:2:4 mix.

office stamp	project		cost index
⊗			**864**
	drawing EXTERNAL WORKS DETAIL Pre-cast concrete kerb		detail number **8.5**
	scale 1:10	approved	date

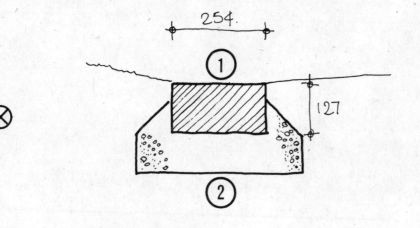

1. Precast concrete channel to BS 340, Figure 8.

2. 100 mm concrete bed and haunching, 1:2:4 mix.

office stamp	project		cost index
⊗			**594**
	drawing EXTERNAL WORKS DETAIL Pre-cast concrete flush kerb		detail number **8.6**
	scale 1:10	approved	date

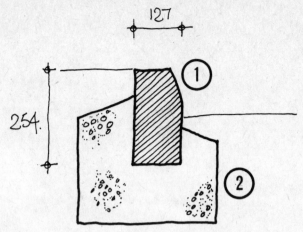

115

127

254.

1. Precast concrete kerb to BS 340
Figure 7 granite aggregate.

2. 150 mm concrete base and surround,
1:2:4 mix.

office stamp	project		cost index
⊗			**776**
	drawing	EXTERNAL WORKS DETAIL Pre-cast concrete kerb	detail number **8·7**
	scale 1:10	approved	date

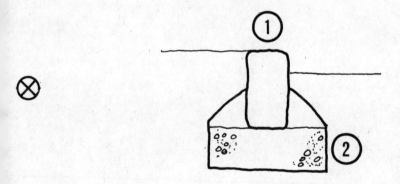

1. 100 x 100 x 200 mm second hand
granite setts. Joints to be mortar
pointed.

2. 100 mm concrete bed and haunching,
1:2:4 mix.

office stamp	project		cost index
⊗			**542**
	drawing	EXTERNAL WORKS DETAIL Granite sett kerb	detail number **8·8**
	scale 1:10	approved	date

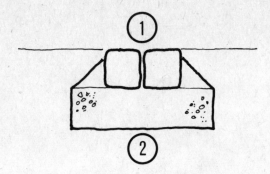

116

1. Double row of 100 x 200 mm granite setts laid breaking bond on 1:3 cement mortar bed.

2. 100 mm concrete foundation and haunching.

⊗

project		cost index **638**
drawing **EXTERNAL WORKS DETAIL** Granite sett trim		detail number **8·9**
scale	approved	date

⊗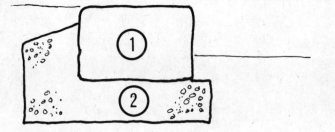

1. 300 x 200 mm granite kerb, to BS 435:1975 Standard dressing B.

2. 100 mm concrete foundation with 150 mm backing.

office stamp

project		cost index **841**
drawing **EXTERNAL WORKS DETAIL** Granite Kerb		detail number **8·10**
scale 1:10	approved	date

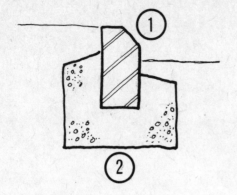

117

1. Single cant engineering brick on end, joints pointed with 1:3 cement mortar.

2. 100 mm concrete foundation and haunching 1:8 mix.

office stamp	project		cost index **734**
⊗	drawing	EXTERNAL WORKS DETAIL Brick kerb	detail number **8·11**
	scale 1:10	approved	date

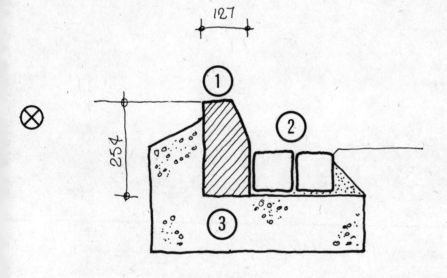

127

254

1. Precast concrete kerb to BS 340 Fig. 7 granite aggregate all joints pointed with 1:3 cement mortar.

2. 2 courses 200 x 100 mm granite setts laid breaking bond on 15 mm 1:3 cement mortar bed, all joints pointed.

3. 150 mm concrete foundation and backing 1:8 mix.

office stamp	project		cost index **1184**
⊗	drawing	EXTERNAL WORKS DETAIL Concrete and granite sett kerb	detail number **8·12**
	scale 1:10	approved	date

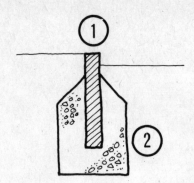

118

1. 50 x 250 mm precast concrete edging.

2. 75 mm concrete surround 1:2:4 mix.

office stamp	project		cost index
⊗			**486**
	drawing	EXTERNAL WORKS DETAIL Pre-cast concrete edging	detail number
			8·13
	scale	approved	date
	1:10		

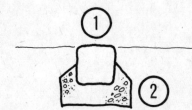

1. Single course second hand 100 x 100 x 100 mm granite setts.

2. 75 mm concrete bed 1:2:4 mix.

office stamp	project		cost index
			476
	drawing	EXTERNAL WORKS DETAIL Granite sett trim	detail number
			8·14
	scale	approved	date
	1:10		

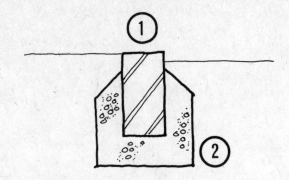

119

1. Engineering brick on end, all joints mortar pointed.

2. 75 mm concrete surround 1:2:4 mix.

office stamp	project		cost index 702
⊗	drawing	EXTERNAL WORKS DETAIL Brick kerb	detail number **8·15**
	scale 1:10	approved	date

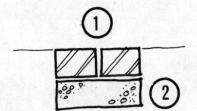

1. Double course engineering brick laid flat breaking joint, all joints mortar pointed.

2. 75 mm concrete bed 1:2:4 mix.

office stamp	project		cost index 516
	drawing	EXTERNAL WORKS DETAIL Brickwork trim	detail number **8·16**
	scale 1:10	approved	date

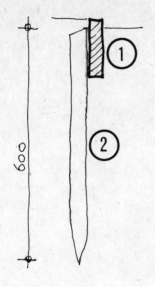

120

1. 150 x 38 mm softwood board pressure impregnated with preservative as specified, nailed to pegs with 65 mm galvanised nails.

2. 50 x 50 mm softwood pegs pressure impregnated with preservative as specified, driven into the ground at 1.2 m centres

office stamp	project		cost index
⊗			**100**
	drawing EXTERNAL WORKS DETAIL Timber board edging		detail number **8·17**
	scale 1:10	approved	date

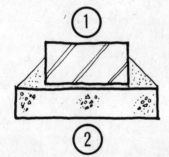

1. Brick on edge on 1:3 cement mortar bed and mortar haunching. All joints mortar pointed.

2. 75 mm concrete foundation 1:2:4 mix.

office stamp	project		cost index
			581
	drawing EXTERNAL WORKS DETAIL Brick on edge edging		detail number **8·18**
	scale 1:10	approved	date

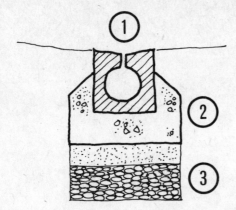

121

1. Precast concrete 'Safeticurb' by
    Charcon Products Ltd.,
    bedded on 1:3 cement mortar, all
    joints pointed up.

2. 100 mm 1:24 concrete bed and
    haunching.

3. 150 mm hardcore blinded with 50 mm
    sand.

office stamp	project		cost index **1072**
⊗	drawing **EXTERNAL WORKS DETAIL** 'Safeticurb' drainage channel		detail number **8·19**
	scale 1:10	approved	date	

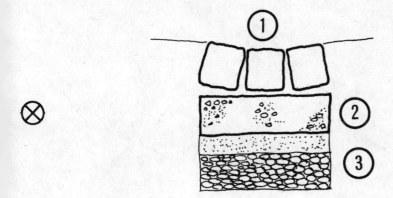

1. 3 no. courses second hand 100 x 100
    granite setts laid to form dished
    channels bedded on 1:3 cement mortar,
    all joints pointed.

2. 100 mm 1:2:4 concrete.

3. 150 mm hardcore blinded with 50 mm
    sand.

office stamp	project		cost index **626**
⊗	drawing **EXTERNAL WORKS DETAIL** Granite sett drainage channel		detail number **8·20**
	scale 1:10	approved	date	

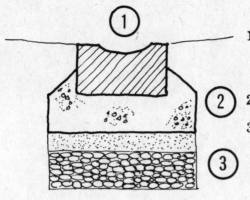

122

1. 250 x 125 mm precast concrete dished channel bedded on 1:3 cement mortar, all joints pointed.

2. 100 mm 1:2:4 concrete bed and haunching.

3. 150 mm hardcore blinded with 50 mm sand.

office stamp ⊗	project	cost index **613**
	drawing EXTERNAL WORKS DETAIL Precast concrete dished channel	detail number **8·21**
	scale 1:10	approved	date	

1. 3 courses engineering brick laid breaking joint to form dished channel, on 1:3 cement mortar bed.   All joints pointed with 1:3 cement mortar.

2. 100 mm 1:2:4: concrete.

3. 150 mm hardcore blinded with 50 mm sand.

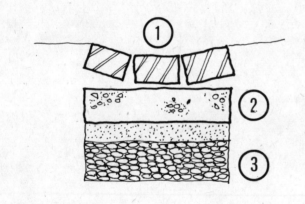

office stamp	project	cost index **808**
	drawing EXTERNAL WORKS DETAIL Brick drainage channel	detail number **8·22**
	scale 1:10	approved	date	

9.0 GATES

Opening Width

For pedestrian use the structural opening width should not be less than 900 mm. Except for special designs (e.g. gallows gates) the maximum leaf size should be 1200 mm. For openings larger than this double gates should be used.

For mower access to protected grass areas, a clear opening width of 2400 mm is required.

Vehicular control of estate roads or parking areas can be effected by the use of gallows gates with opening widths of up to 5200 mm.

Height

Gate height should be equal to or slightly lower than the adjacent enclosure.

Hinges, Locks and Latches

Hinges

The usual type of gate hinge is the steel band hinge. There are two basic types:

1). hook and band

2). reversible

Hook and band are available as light or heavy duty, straight or cranked.

Reversible hinges are available as light or heavy duty.

Both types are available hot dip galvanized or sherardized.

Tee hinges are also used. These are usually available in a japanned finish but can be specially ordered with a galvanized finish.

All hinge types are described in BS 1227 pt 1A 1967.

Locks

Locks for gates usually take the form of barrel bolts. Where these are secured with a padlock they are called padbolts.

Double gates should be fitted with bolts to engage in sockets set in concrete or tarmac.

125

A centre stop should be used in conjunction with the bolts. These can be of the fall-down type if the passage of lawn mowers is anticipated.

Provision should be made for securing gates in the open position, either by the provision of an additional bolt socket or a cabin hook and eye.

Latches

The type of gate latch fitted will depend on the gate height. Low gates can be fitted with automatic gate latch fitted to the inside of the gate only. High gates can be fitted with a Suffolk type of thumb latch or a Ring Handle Gate Latch which are both operable from either side of the gate. BS 1331 describes latches suitable for gates.

Construction

The main point about gate construction is to ensure that adequate cross bracing is provided to prevent the gate dropping.

The usual method of achieving this with timber construction is to provide a diagonal brace from the bottom corner on the hinge side so that the brace is in compression.

Tall gates are provided with two separate braces. Metal gates of bolted construction are braced in the same manner. Welded metal gates are not usually cross braced.

Gate stops should be provided. The latch should not be relied on to stop the gate. Double gates should be provided with rebated meeting stiles.

REFERENCES

British Standards Institute
  BS 4092 Domestic Front Entrance Gates
    Part 1 : 1966 Metal Gates
    Part 2 : 1966 Wooden Gates

BS 1331 Builders Hardware for Housing
  Schedule 1 : Door and gate equipment

9.0   GATES

9.1   Low match board gate
9.2   Low timber palisade gate
9.3   High match board gate
9.4   Double gates 1.8 m high

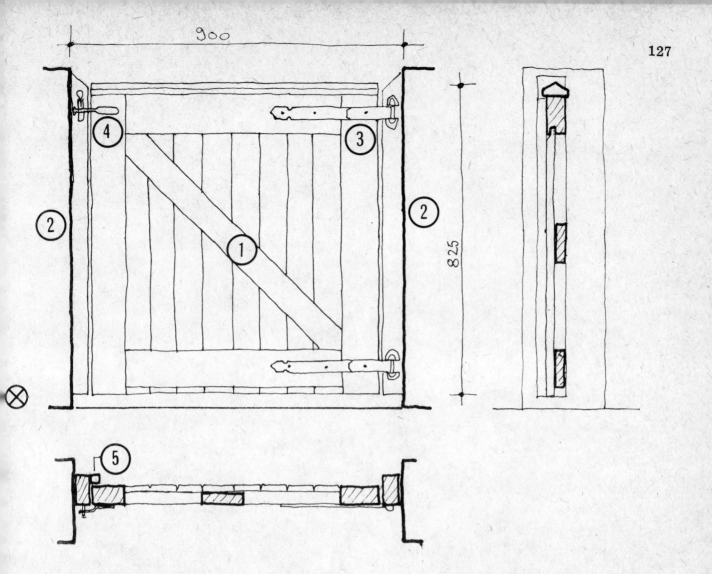

127

1. Softwood framed ledged and braced gate, construction and dimensions of members to BS 459 pt 4 with twice weathered hardwood capping fixed with galvanized nails. Paint finish.

2. 44 x 69 mm s.w gate posts with weathered top end bolted to brickwork with 2 no. 10 mm x 100 mm Rawlbolts. Paint finish.

3. 1 pair 300 mm light reversible hinge to BS 1227 pt 1A galvanized finish. 35 mm sherardized screw fixing.

4. Automatic gate latch galvanized finish, 25 mm sherardized screw fixing.

5. 19 x 19 mm s.w gate stop. 35 mm sherardized screw fixing. Paint finish.

NOTE: Timber to be vacuum impregnated with preservative as specified.

office stamp	project			cost index **103**
	drawing	EXTERNAL WORKS DETAIL Low matchboard gate		detail number **9·1**
	scale 1:10	approved	date	

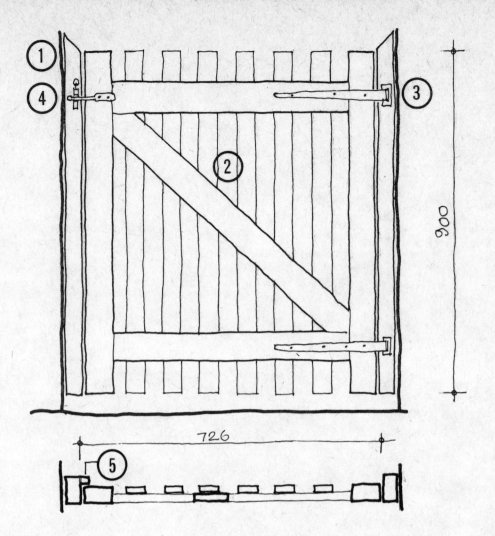

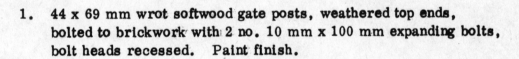

128

1. 44 x 69 mm wrot softwood gate posts, weathered top ends, bolted to brickwork with 2 no. 10 mm x 100 mm expanding bolts, bolt heads recessed.   Paint finish.

2. Wrot softwood gate constructed in accordance with BS 4092, pt 2, 1966.   Pales to be 19 mm x 71 mm wrot softwood fixed at 100 mm centres.

3. 1 pair 300 mm galvanized mild steel tee hinges to BS 1227. 35 mm sherardized screw fixing.

4. Automatic gate latch, galvanized finish 25 mm sherardized screw fixing.

5. 25 x 25 mm softwood planted gate stop.   50 mm sherardized screw fixing 450 mm centres.

office stamp	project		cost index
			100
	drawing EXTERNAL WORKS DETAIL Low timber palisade gate		detail number
			9·2
	scale 1:10	approved date	

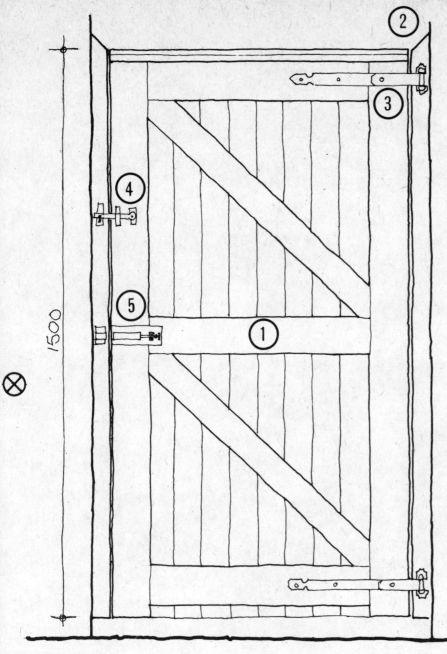

129

1. Softwood framed ledged braced door construction and dimensions of members to BS 459, pt 4, with twice weathered hardwood capping fixed with galvanized nails. Paint finish.

2. 44 x 69 mm wrot softwood gate posts with weathered top end bolted to brickwork with 4 no. 10 mm x 100 mm expanding bolts with washers. Bolt heads to be recessed.

3. 1 pair 300 mm light reversible hinge to BS 1227, pt 1A, galvanised finish. 35 mm sherardized screw fixing.

4. Heavy duty Suffolk latch galvanized finish.

5. 203 mm heavy duty barrel bolt galvanized finish.

6. 25 x 25 mm softwood gate stop. 35 mm sherardized screw fixing. 450 mm centres. Paint finish.

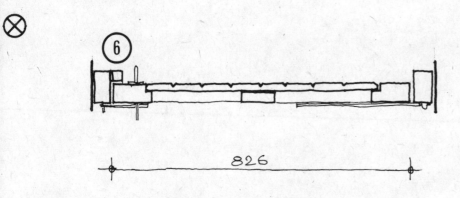

826

office stamp	project		cost index
			164
	drawing EXTERNAL WORKS DETAIL High match board gate		detail number
			9·3
	scale 1:10	approved	date

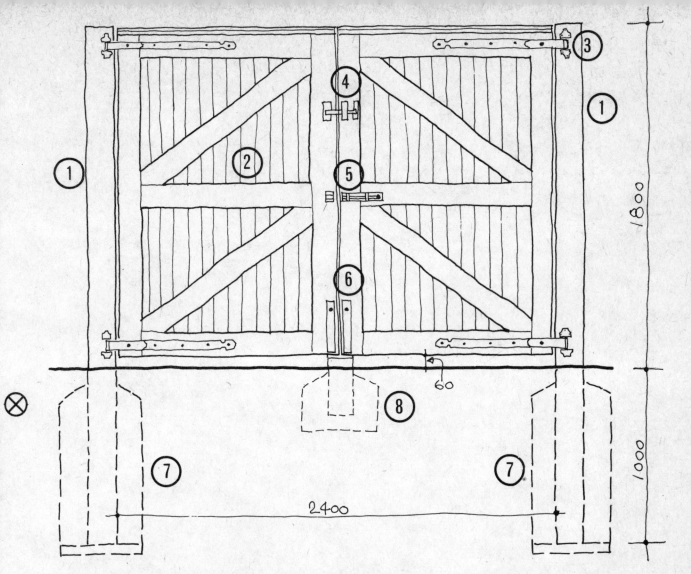

1. 150 x 150 mm sawn oak gate post. 2800 mm long. Buried end to be creosote impregnated as specified.

2. Framed ledged and braced double leaf softwood gate. Generally as BS 459 pt 4 but stiles and top rail to be 119 x 59 mm and middle rail braces and bottom rail to be 119 x 34 mm. Twice weathered hardwood capping fixed with galvanized nails.

3. 686 mm heavy steel reversible hinge to BS 1227 pt 1A. Galvanized finish sherardized screw and bolt fixed.

4. Heavy duty Suffolk latch galvanized finish.

5. 203 mm heavy duty padbolt galvanized finish complete with padlock.

6. 2 no. 381 cross pattern galvanized bolts.

7. 450 x 450 mm concrete surround to post 1:8 mix.

8. 150 x 150 mm sawn oak stop set in 400 x 400 x 300 mm concrete.

office stamp	project		cost index
			1131
	drawing EXTERNAL WORKS DETAIL Double gates 1.8 m high		detail number
			9.4
	scale 1:20	approved	date

132

10.0   SOILING, TURFING AND SEEDING

Soiling

The supply and placing to topsoil is usually the responsibility of the Main Contractor, and must be approved by the Architect before placing.

Topsoil is specified by reference to BS 3882, the main aspects being texture, soil reaction and stone content.

Where topsoil from site stripping is re-used it is important to ensure that it is free from builder debris, subsoil, large stones and weeds and that it has been stored properly on site.

Turfing

Turfing is specified by reference to BS 4428 : 1969.   Turfing, including the final preparation of the topsoil, can either be carried out by the Main Contractor or by a nominated Landscape Subcontractor.   Because turf can be laid satisfactorily at any season (except exceptionally dry or frosty weather), it is usual practice to allow the Main Contractor to carry out the turfing, so that the topsoil is protected until the next planting season.

Some authorities ask for shrub areas to be turfed if the building handover does not coincide with the correct planting season.

The turf shall be maintained by cutting and watering by the main contractor or the nominated Landscape Subcontractor until handover and after handover until the expiration of the Defects Liability Period, (which ideally should be 12 months).

Seeding

Seeding, including the cultivation and fertilizing of the topsoil is usually carried out by a nominated Landscape Subcontractor.   The Architect must specify the grass seed mixture by reference to BS 4428 : 1969, the main difference between the mixtures being the inclusion or otherwise of Rygrass. Grass from seed containing Rygrass has enhanced wearing qualities.

Sowing of grass seed is best carried out from July to October.   Sowing can be carried out by hand or machine at a rate of 45 gm/m^2.   After sowing the ground should be raked or harrowed and then lightly rolled.

Grass areas grown from seed should not be certified practically complete until it is evident that germination over the whole area has occurred satisfactorily, all weeds have been removed and a good sward is obtained.

133

REFERENCES

E and F. N. Spon Ltd.
Spon's Landscape Handbook

British Standard Institute
BS 4428 1969 Recommendations for general
landscape operations
BS 3969 1965 Recommendations for turf for
general Landscape Work
BS 3882 1965 Recommendations and
classification for topsoil

South London Consortium
Soft Landscaping Specification

10.0 SOILING, TURFING AND SEEDING

10.1 Grass turfed areas
10.2 Grass seeded areas
10.3 Planted areas
10.4 Climber pit
10.5 Tree pit

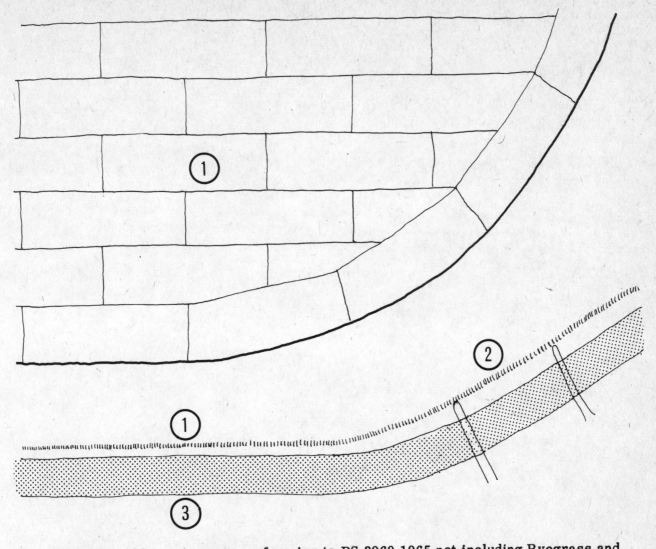

1. 300 x 900 x 25 mm turves, conforming to BS 3969:1965 not including Ryegrass and laid stretcher bond, breaking joints in accordance with BS 4428:1969. All margins and edges are to be laid with whole turves as shown.

2. Turves on banks exceeding 30° shall be laid parallel to the contours, and each turf shall be secured by 2 no 4 mm diameter galvanized wire pins, 200 mm long.

3. 100 mm top soil, conforming with BS 3882 (medium loam with a maximum 20% of stones), where imported. Top soil shall be free of all weeds and rubbish, brought to a fine tilth, and lightly and uniformly firmed.

office stamp	project		cost index
			113
	drawing		detail number
	EXTERNAL WORKS DETAIL		
	Grass turfed areas		**10·1**
	scale	approved	date
	1:10		

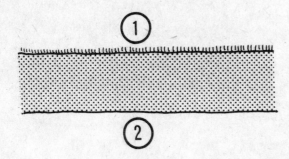

136

1. Grass seed conforming to BS 4428, the mixture to be as specified. Seed shall be sown at a density of 45 gm/m².

2. 150 mm top soil conforming with BS 3882, brought to a fine tilth and lightly and uniformly firmed.

office stamp	project		cost index
⊗			**100**
	drawing **EXTERNAL WORKS DETAIL** Grass seeded areas		detail number **10·2**
	scale 1:10	approved	date

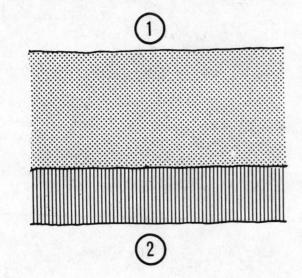

1. 300 mm topsoil conforming with BS 3882, medium loam with 20% maximum of stones.

2. 150 mm broken up ground with all large stones, builder's debris, etc removed.

office stamp	project		cost index
⊗			**182**
	drawing **EXTERNAL WORKS DETAIL** Planted areas		detail number **10·3**
	scale 1:10	approved	date

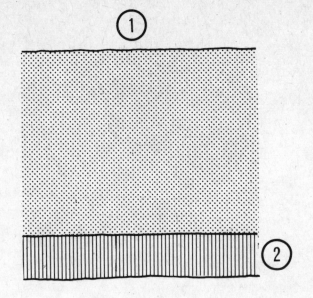

137

1. 450 mm deep excavation 600 mm square filled with lightly consolidated top soil conforming with BS 3882. Medium loam 20% maximum stones.

2. 150 mm broken up bottom to the excavation. All large stones, builders debris etc to be removed.

office stamp	project	cost index
⊗		**303**
	drawing EXTERNAL WORKS DETAIL Climber pit	detail number **10.4**
	scale 1:10	approved	date	

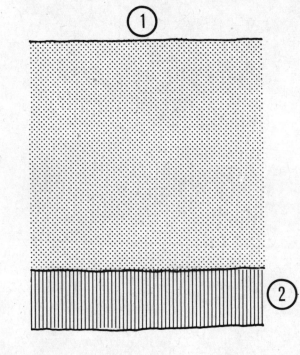

1. 600 mm deep excavation 1000 mm square filled with lightly consolidated top soil conforming with BS 3882. Medium loam 20% maximum stones.

2. 150 mm broken up bottom to excavation. All large stones, builders debris etc to be removed.

office stamp	project	cost index
		398
	drawing EXTERNAL WORKS DETAIL Tree pit	detail number **10.5**
	scale 1:10	approved	date	

138

11.00   TREE SURROUNDS

Size

Size should be between 1.2 m and 1.5 m square to enable excavation of the tree pit after placing the edging.

Edging

The edging can be any of the edgings described in Section 8, its function being to retain the paving on the outside of the tree surround.

Care is required when working around existing trees to choose an edging which will not damage any roots which may be close to the surface.   If necessary no edging need be used, the paving being changed to a rigid unit type in the vicinity of the tree.

Edgings are usually flush with the surrounding pavings to enable the surface run-off to drain into the tree surround.

Infill Material

The infill material should be porous to enable surface run-off to water the tree.   The material should be lightly compacted by hand.   Rigid units should be bedded on sand and joints should be unfilled or filled with sand.

When using rigid units as infill, a hole of about 450 mm square should be left free for the tree trunk.

When working around existing trees, the ground should not be excavated at all around the tree, the infill material being placed on the hand compacted topsoil.

Cast iron tree grids should be supported off the ground by the edging or can be bedded on sand as paving.

Perforated concrete slabs should be bedded on sand.

REFERENCES

E and F. N. Spon Ltd.
  Spon's Landscape Handbook

140

11.0   TREE SURROUNDS

11.1   Hoggin tree surround
11.2   Cast iron tree surround

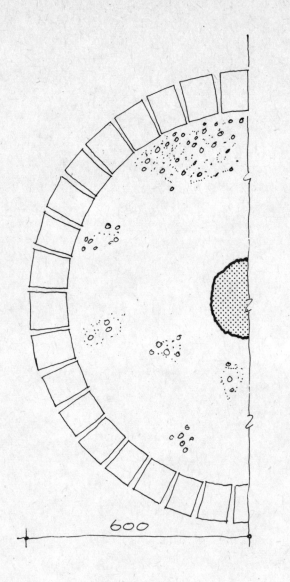

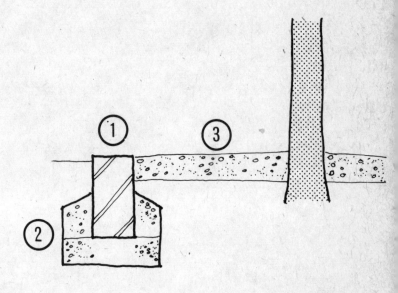

600

1. Brick on end surround.

2. 75 mm 1:6 concrete surround.

3. 50 mm hand consolidated coarse hoggin.

office stamp	project		cost index **100**
	drawing	EXTERNAL WORKS DETAIL Hoggin tree surround	detail number **11·1**
	scale 1:10	approved	date	